# more annie stories

## Therapeutic Storytelling Techniques

Doris Brett

Foreword by
Jeffrey K. Zeig, Ph.D.

Magination Press ~ New York

Library of Congress Cataloging-in-Publication Data
Brett, Davis.
    More Annie stories : therapeutic storytelling
techniques / Doris Brett.
        p.  cm.
    Includes bibliographical references.
    ISBN 0-945354-47-9
        1. Child psychology.   2. Parenting.   3. Storytelling.
    4. Children's stories.   I. Title.
    HQ772.B693   1992
    808.5'43—dc20                                      91-46084
                                                           CIP

Chapters 9, Divorce, and 13, Relaxation, are reprinted with permission from *Annie Stories*, by Doris Brett, Workman Publishing Company, Inc., New York, 1988.

Published by Magination Press, an imprint of Brunner/Mazel, Inc., 19 Union Square West, New York, NY 10003; 1-800-825-3089.

Distributed in Canada by Book Center, 1140 Beaulac St., Montreal, Quebec H4R 1R8, Canada

Manufactured in the United States of America

10 9 8 7 6 5 4 3 2 1

For Martin and Amantha, with much love

# Contents

Foreword................................................................. vii

1. Introduction .................................................. 1
2. How to Use and Tell Annie Stories............................ 15
3. How to Teach Annie Stories .................................. 21
4. Fear of the Dark............................................. 34
   ANNIE STORY ................................................. 36
5. Bedwetting................................................... 44
   ANNIE STORY ................................................. 48
6. Compulsive and Perfectionistic Children..................... 65
   ANNIE STORY #1 .............................................. 69
   ANNIE STORY #2 .............................................. 82
7. Shyness ..................................................... 92
   ANNIE STORY ................................................. 94
8. Teasing...................................................... 108
   ANNIE STORY ................................................. 109
9. Divorce ..................................................... 118
   ANNIE STORY ................................................. 132
10. Stepfamilies ............................................... 147
    ANNIE STORY ................................................ 151
11. Impulsive Children ......................................... 166
    ANNIE STORY ................................................ 170
12. Siblings.................................................... 179
    ANNIE STORY ................................................ 182
13. Children of Alcoholics ..................................... 189
    ANNIE STORY ................................................ 192

*v*

# Contents

14. **Relaxation** ............................................................ 203
     Annie Story ................................................... 205

**Resources** ............................................................ 214
**Further Reading** ................................................... 214

# Foreword

I first met Doris Brett—clinical psychologist, consultant, and author of international renown—more than six years ago, when she attended training workshops I led on Ericksonian psychotherapy for health professionals in Melbourne, Australia, her home city. Later we renewed our acquaintance when she presented her work in San Francisco in 1988 at a Congress for psychotherapists on Brief Therapy organized by The Milton H. Erickson Foundation.

In addition to *More Annie Stories: Therapeutic Storytelling Techniques*, Brett has authored a previous volume, *Annie Stories: A Special Kind of Storytelling*; an award-winning collection of poetry, *The Truth About Unicorns*; a book on baking, *Doris Brett's Australian Bread Book*; and a novel, *Looking for Unicorns*. During a promotional tour in the United States in 1989, she was interviewed on the *Today Show* and on numerous radio programs.

Underlying all of Brett's impressive personal achievements is her marvelous ability as a storyteller. She has an uncanny knack for making essential ideas sound simple, and for making these ideas come alive through the magic of engaging anecdotes.

In *More Annie Stories*, Doris Brett continues to address her storytelling talents to parents who want to help their children solve problems. She constructs stories especially for parents to tell their youngsters. There are stories on eleven topics, including dealing with siblings, divorce, stepfamilies, shyness, and impulsiveness. Brett explains how parents can tailor the tales for their own children. She also points out the therapeutic reasoning behind the storylines.

I have used Doris Brett's method with my own daughter and found it most effective. This kind of storytelling provides a powerful method for helping children surmount personal problems.

Why does this anecdotal method work? It is because it speaks the language of the child and enters into the child's own world. Stories create an *experience* of change. Children (like adults!) are influenced more profoundly by experiences than by verbal object lessons. A frustrated parent can explain endlessly the importance of keeping one's room clean or the reason thumbsucking is bad; however, such "lecturing" does not contain much power to effect change. Yet, when ideas are "gift wrapped" in the form of a story, they become energized. When children "unwrap" the "gift" and discover inherent meaning in the story, they access their own ability to change. Parents will see delight on their children's faces as they grasp the ideas in the stories. And behavioral change will follow.

Of course, some metaphors can impede change instead of foster it. For example, parables that preach and the heavy-handed lectures of the moralist leave no room for discovery and can promote resistance. Note the sensitive tone in Brett's metaphors. Her stories are gifts for the troubled young soul. Whether the problems are common—like being teased—or more intractable—like compulsive and perfectionistic behavior—Annie Stories can help boys and girls find a way out of the binds that confine them.

Parenting is one of the joys of life. It can also be one of life's trials. Sometimes it is difficult to know how to reach our children or how to help them bring out their best. It is good we have experts like Doris Brett, who provide powerful and easy-to-use tools to make parenting easier.

—JEFFREY K. ZEIG, Ph.D.
*Director, The Milton H. Erickson Foundation*
*Phoenix, Arizona, USA*
*December 1991*

# 1

## Introduction

Annie Stories started for me about ten years ago. They started because my then three-year-old daughter, Amantha, was shy. This fact later caused ripples of amusement among various interviewers as I plowed through a publicity tour for my first book on Annie Stories. Inevitably the opening question would be, "And how did Annie Stories begin?" I would say, "They began because Amantha was shy." Amantha was by this time a distinctly un-shy ten-year-old. As the interviewers watched her delicately maneuver the microphone away from Mom so as to have more "air time," you could see the disbelief in their faces.

However, at three, Amantha was shy. She was very cautious in unfamiliar surroundings. At play group, she was the last child to leave the security of her mother's lap and venture out to play. While the other children charged happily around, Amantha sat by my ankles regarding the scene with a mixture of amazement and horror. The other mothers looked pityingly at me. The words "And she's a psychologist, too" were clearly illuminated in thought bubbles above their heads.

With this as background, I knew that the idea of nursery school would not have sparkling appeal for Amantha. So my husband and I spent a lot of time talking to her about nursery school. We wanted to reassure her that it would be fine, that she would be safe, that she would enjoy it, and so on. We reassured her, in fact, until we were blue in the face. She listened, she looked at us, and we realized that despite the brilliant case we were making for the joys of nursery school, Amantha was not going to be reassured. Her look plainly said, "Well, nursery school might be fine for you guys, but not for me."

It was at this point that I had the idea of telling Amantha a story.

The story was about a little girl called Annie. Annie lived in a house just like ours. She had a dog just like ours. She had a daddy and mommy just like Martin and me. Most importantly, she had a problem—she was frightened of going to nursery school. The story followed Annie through her first day at nursery school, where she discovered it wasn't quite as bad as she thought it would be, and on through succeeding days. With each day, Annie enjoyed nursery school more and more. By the end of the first week she was having a great time.

Amantha was riveted by the story. She asked for it again and again. By the time nursery school actually came around, Amantha coped with it well, just as Annie had in the story.

I was struck by the success of the storytelling method, but Amantha was even more struck by it. From then on, every time she was scared of something or wrestling with a conflict, she would come to me and say, "Tell me an Annie Story." And I would tell her a story about how Annie coped with a similar difficulty. Each time the result was the same. Amantha asked for the story again and again and then went on to deal with her problem far more confidently and successfully than she'd been able to before.

I began teaching other parents how to tell Annie Stories. Therapists and teachers were also interested in learning the technique. By the time the first book of Annie Stories had been published, I had a wealth of positive feedback from both parents and professionals. Children loved hearing the stories. They felt comforted and strengthened by them. They were able to use the stories to help them face fears and understand and resolve conflicts. The parents enjoyed telling the stories. They felt empowered by them. Instead of feeling helpless in the face of their child's distress, they were now able to do something. And furthermore, that something was simple, natural, sensible, and didn't require a Ph.D. in clinical psychology.

## How Children Learn

Stories and children are like bacon and eggs—they just go together. All over the world, through myriad different cultures and lifestyles, storytelling time attracts an audience of wide-eyed and entranced children.

There are good reasons for this.

As adults, if we want to learn about something, we have many options available to us. We can go to the library or a bookstore and read about it. We can consult experts in the field for their opinions. We can track down newspaper articles or journals. We can attend lectures or seminars. We can talk to friends and share information and ideas.

All of the above require certain adult skills—the ability to read and research material, the ability to verbalize one's thoughts and ideas, the ability to conceptualize and communicate at a fairly sophisticated level.

These adult skills have been learned, sometimes painfully, over many years. They are not innate—that is, children are not born knowing how to talk, reason things out, and arrive at logical conclusions. And yet they have a great deal to learn about the world. Faced with this lack of adult learning skills, how do they do it?

The answer is through play and imagination. Games of "drop the rattle" teach babies about the laws of gravity. Games of peek-a-boo teach them that objects, and in particular mothers, have a stable existence in this world. Games of make-believe allow them to discover what it feels like to be a mommy or a daddy or a wild terrifying tiger. Imaginary companions provide them with a way of sounding out feelings and exploring different options.

For the young of all species, the world is new. It needs to be explored, discovered, learned, and mastered. Fortunately, young human beings are born with an overpowering drive to do this. Watch the persistence with which an infant learns to walk. She[1] pulls herself up and falls down on her face, pulls herself up and falls again, over and over. Sir Edmund Hilary couldn't have shown more grit and determination in his assault on Mount Everest.

As another example, watch the way a baby will keep dropping her favorite toy over the side of her high chair. Her curiosity and

---

[1]Since this is a book of Annie stories, I have used the feminine pronoun throughout to stand for both girls and boys.

need to learn more about the rules of her world are so intense that she is willing to risk losing a precious possession. This is equivalent to a scientist testing out a time travel machine with his newly acquired Porsche. Will the Porsche make it back from the future? Most scientists would have to feel pretty sure of their invention to be willing to take that chance. Babies are much more adventurous scientists. They're willing to risk a great deal in their quest for knowledge.

Remember, this quest for learning is undertaken through the means of play and imagination. Play provides a way of practicing skills that must be mastered by adulthood. Play is, in effect, the youngsters' equivalent of work and study.

If you watch children play, you will notice that a great deal of their play consists of imitation. They imitate mothers and fathers, older siblings, TV heroes, and so on. This imitative behavior makes good survival sense. Since most of the skills necessary for human life are too complex to be installed as instincts, these skills must be learned through on-the-job training. We watch someone doing something, and then we do it ourselves. In other words, we imitate people who have already mastered what we need to know. Children's strong drive to imitate helps them learn the complicated ins and outs of adult human behavior.

Studies have shown that when children are offered a choice of two models to imitate—one successful and the other unsuccessful—they imitate the successful model. Annie Stories make good use of this propensity. Annie, in learning to deal with her problems, becomes a successful model, thus encouraging the child to imitate her success.

Studies of storytelling as a modeling technique have also shown that the more closely a story's setting and imagery coincide with the listener's real life situation, the more likely it is that the message of the story will be absorbed and acted upon. Again, Annie Stories take advantage of this finding.

Play and imagination, therefore, allow the child to explore and understand her world in a variety of ways. She can test out and practice various roles—discover what it feels like to be the cop as well as the robber, the mother as well as the baby. She can use imagination as a way of exploring and mastering feelings. She can discover different aspects of herself and begin to learn about new and unfamiliar elements of her world.

## Communicating Through Stories

We know that from the beginning, children use play and imagination as their natural ways of learning, exploring, and understanding. Therefore, when we want to teach a child or communicate something of importance to her, it makes sense to do it in a way that can be recognized, digested, and understood by her. If we wanted to explain complicated issues to a French person, we would, after all, get much further if we spoke in French. In just the same way, when you talk to children through stories, you are talking to them in the language they understand and respond to best—that of fantasy and imagination.

Stories have always been a powerful way of communicating with children. Fairy stories are a prime example. They have been handed down through the ages and echoed through many different cultures. In his book, *The Uses of Enchantment*, Bruno Bettelheim explained that fairy tales play a powerful role in helping children come to terms with the various anxieties and conflicts they encounter.

Fairy tales deal with issues that are important to children. "Cinderella," for instance, is concerned with sibling rivalry. "Hansel and Gretel" focuses on the fear of being abandoned. "Tom Thumb" speaks of the terror, helplessness, and frustration of finding yourself in a world where everything is overwhelmingly bigger and more powerful than you. Fairy tales explore the themes of good versus bad, of altruism versus avarice, courage versus cowardice, kindness versus cruelty, perseverance versus giving up. They teach the child that the world is a complex place, that things happen that seem unfair and unjustified, that the odds against success may seem overwhelming at times, that fear, regret, and despair are as much a part of our world as joy, optimism, and confidence. But most importantly, they also teach the child that if you can just keep going, even though the situation looks hopeless, if you can stick to your moral standards, even though temptation beckons at every corner, eventually you will win.

As children hear these stories, they recognize at an unconscious level the echoes that resonate in their own lives. They can use the stories to work through some of their own fears and feelings about these issues. They are also given the message of hope. This is a very important message. A child who does not have hope will give up the struggle and never succeed.

## How Annie Stories Work

Annie Stories are like personalized fairy stories. They involve a heroine or hero who mirrors the characteristics of your child and who is also facing the same kinds of problems that your child is facing. In the Annie Story, the heroine/hero finds ways of understanding and resolving these difficulties and conflicts. In addition to real life characters, the stories may involve magic and fantasy characters. The protagonists may be baby bunnies or junior hippopotami. The basic ingredient is that the personality and problems of the protagonist match that of your child. The story is adapted to suit your child just as the protagonist's name is. I called my stories Annie Stories because my daughter's name is Amantha. I wanted a heroine whose name was similar to Amantha's but not identical. If I had been telling these stories to a boy named Jack, for instance, I might have called them Joey Stories.

Annie Stories help children deal with the situations or emotions that are worrying them. They don't provide a magic wand to whisk away all the trouble and pain of the real world, but they do allow children to learn about themselves and their problems in a way that makes them feel comforted, supported, strengthened, and understood.

There are many reasons why Annie Stories work so well.

First, the Annie Story enables your child to think about and confront her problems in a way that is not threatening. Many children feel guilty or embarrassed about their worries. They find it difficult to talk about them openly. Often, if you start to talk directly to them about these problems, they will clam up and retreat. Listening to a story, however, is a whole different ball game. The child is not being lectured at, accused, or pressured to talk about difficulties—she is simply listening to a story about a girl just like her. She is free to listen, learn, and make connections in a way that feels safe. This means she is able to listen to and think about material that might be too anxiety arousing for her in other circumstances. By changing the context, you have created a safety zone.

There is a wonderful joke that illustrates the importance of context. A man is in court suing for damages as a result of a car accident. A lawyer is cross-examining him.

"Now, Mr. Brown," he says, "will you tell the court what happened on the morning of February 12th."

Mr. Brown replies, "I was driving along a country road when a bolting horse galloped in front of my car. I swerved but couldn't avoid the horse. The impact of the collision with the horse sent the car skidding into a field where it hit a cow. I was then thrown out and lost consciousness briefly."

"Very well," says the lawyer, "and is it not true that when you recovered consciousness, the local veterinarian had arrived at the scene. He bent over you and asked how you were feeling. You replied, 'I've never felt better in my life.'"

"That is true," says Mr. Brown.

"Then," thunders the lawyer, "how do you have the temerity to come before this court claiming damages for physical disability as a result of this accident?"

"Well," says Mr. Brown, "let me explain. When I recovered consciousness, I found I was lying in a field in excruciating pain. I saw the vet arrive. He walked over to the horse, which was lying groaning on the roadway. He looked at the horse, took out a gun, and shot the horse. He walked over to the cow, which lay on the grass. He looked at the cow, took out his gun, and shot the cow. He then walked over to me and asked how I was feeling. I replied that I'd never felt better in my life."

An Annie Story enables your child to think about, wonder about, and ask questions about conflict-laden areas without fear of being shot down. It is something that we, as adults, also do. Most of us have had the experience of getting advice about an embarrassing problem through the "My friend John has a problem . . ." technique.

The way children make use of this safety zone is interesting. Most of the time the child is perfectly aware that Annie is really herself. However, when the material gets threatening, she switches to pretending that Annie is just a girl in a story. Thus, she is able to keep listening instead of having to back away or shut down.

The story framework also has the advantage of being more interesting for a child than a lecture. All over the world, children turn off at lectures and turn on at story time.

When I was writing the relaxation story for the first book of Annie Stories, I began by working out a relaxation "script" that would be suitable for children. Having polished this up, I decided to test-drive it, as usual, on my daughter. I waited till she was in a suitably grumpy mood before pouncing and saying in my most helpful voice, "Would you like me to help you relax?" Amantha gave me a pained look and I began the relaxation script. At the end of it, Amantha gave a dismissive snort and said, "Boring." I realized then that Amantha had seen my intervention as an imposition. She had been in an irritable, uncooperative mood and didn't want to be told to do anything by anybody. I went back to the drawing board and incorporated the relaxation script into an Annie Story, weaving the script in and out of the story.

Again I waited until Amantha was in an irritable mood. This time, instead of "Would you like me to help you relax?," I said, "Would you like me to tell you a story?"

Amantha nodded, and I began into the story. She listened with rapt attention, spontaneously entering into the relaxation images along with Annie. At the end of the story, she was beaming as she pronounced it "Ace"—the highest accolade an Australian schoolchild at that time could bestow.

The relaxation script had been exactly the same as the one she had pronounced boring. The only difference was that this time it had been couched in the form of a story. She had not felt that it was being pushed at her and had therefore felt free to take it.

Another important thing that happens through the stories is that your child is able to recognize that she is not alone in her fears or feelings; other children feel like this, too. This is immensely reassuring. The child is able to feel normal again instead of feeling that she is a freak—abnormally stupid, wicked, or cowardly, for instance. This reassurance adds to her self-esteem and confidence and will help her work her way through her difficulty.

One of the beneficial aspects of the storytelling technique is that in order to make up and tell the story, the storyteller has to enter empathically into the child's world. In other words, the storyteller has to make an effort to see what things look like from the child's point of view. This is something we don't do nearly enough. We are so used to our adult perspective that we forget there is any other way of looking at things. We forget that, to a child, the monsters in the cupboard are as real as you or me. We forget that magic is as wholeheartedly believed in as electricity or magnetism. We forget that what seems trivial to us may be experienced as devastating from the child's point of view. We forget that our interpretations of events may be totally different from those of the child. This applies even to the way we use language. For example, it's common for adults to say "We've lost Grandma" as a way of saying "Grandma's dead." Children unfamiliar with this euphemism will take it literally—they will interpret your words as meaning that Grandma has wandered off or been somehow mislaid. They may be deeply puzzled by the fact that amidst all the grief, no one is bothering to search for her. They may expect her to find her way back any day.

Because we don't take the trouble to imagine the world through our children's eyes, we frequently end up talking over them and denying their reality. To the child who is scared of the monsters in the dark we say, "Don't be silly, there are no such things as monsters." This makes the child feel stupid and misunderstood as well as frightened. She is even less likely to be able to muster her resources to deal with her monsters. It also drives a wedge between parent and child, as the child feels that the parent does not understand her. It makes future communication harder—if there seems no hope of being understood, why bother trying?

When, however, the parent tells an Annie Story—a story told from the child's point of view and echoing her reality—the child has the opposite experience. She feels understood and validated. It is an enormously comforting feeling for her. It enhances the loving bonds between parent and child. Think back to the last time you had a conversation with someone who really seemed to be on your wavelength, who seemed to understand your feelings and know where you were coming from. Remember how good it felt and how you missed it when it wasn't there?

An Annie Story also enables the child to realize that there are ways of coping with a problem like hers. She can use Annie's successful coping as a model for her own. It gives her hope. If this little girl, who is so like her, can cope, maybe she can, too. She is also able to learn new skills and strategies from hearing about Annie's skills and strategies.

Annie Stories enhance communication in a very special way. Often children are not able to talk about their problems. Sometimes it's because they are ashamed or afraid of what might happen if they do. Sometimes they don't have the words or even the concepts with which to describe their feelings. Hearing their often confused or ambiguous feelings named and put into words through the medium of the story can be extremely helpful. As well as adding clarity to the turmoil inside, naming feelings can also give the child an extra sense of mastery over those feelings.

The Annie Story also gives you an opportunity to have a dialogue with your child. Having a heart-to-heart talk with a child about her worries can sometimes feel like debriefing a captive in a prisoner-of-war camp—name, rank, and serial number are all you get. The same child, however, can be surprisingly open when she's telling you about what's worrying Annie. Again, it's that feeling of safety that allows her to be so revealing. So, if you're not sure what's worrying your child, you can ask her what she thinks Annie's worried about. When I wasn't sure what my daughter was concerned about, I would simply ask her what she would like me to tell her an Annie Story about. If she said something like, "Tell me about Annie going to the doctor," then I would know where the problem lay.

One of the most valuable features of communication through storytelling is that the child who learns through this method is able to do so with a sense of autonomy. She is able to take as much time as she needs to digest the contents and message of the story. She is able to hear the story over and over again to familiarize herself with what may be new or threatening concepts. She is able to approach them with as much caution or urgency as she needs. She is free to focus on whatever element of the story is appropriate to her at any particular moment—nothing is being forced down her throat. And most importantly, whatever learning she gains, she experiences as her own. If she decides to conquer a fear in the manner that Annie does, she does so because she thought of doing it, not because her mommy told her to do it. Thus, the child is able to experience a sense of her own personal power, her ability to think over a situation and decide what to do about it. This is much more strengthening for a child than being in the more helpless and powerless position of having to depend on someone else to solve her problems for her.

I had a very interesting example of this sense of autonomy with my daughter Amantha. She was eleven, an age when she was keen to prove that mommy doesn't always know best. The idea of following mommy's advice had a distinctly babyish, and therefore wimpish, tinge for her. She had come home from school quite upset. In response to my questions, she gave me a cross look and snapped, "No one will play with me." Translated, this turned out to mean that her best friend had decided to no longer be her best friend. I started to offer some good, commonsense advice about what to do when your best friend won't play with you, but Amantha cut me off at the pass. Advice from me was the last thing she wanted.

That evening, I tucked a still-grumpy Amantha into bed. She was obviously still upset over the incident and not looking forward to school the next day. Tentatively, I said to her, "Would you like me to tell you an Annie Story?" She rolled her eyes with an "if you must" expression, and I launched into the story of what Annie did when her best friend wouldn't play with her. Amantha listened with a pained look on her face, and when I finished, she announced crossly, "That was a stupid story and I feel worse than before."

I left the room feeling more inept than when I had entered it. Perhaps, I mused, I was right in thinking that the cut-off age for these stories was ten.

The next day, I picked Amantha up from school with some trepidation. To my surprise, in place of the frowning no-one-will-play-with-me face of yesterday was her familiar cheerful grin.

"Hi," I said. "How was school today?"

"Fine," she said.

Encouraged, I inquired about the social scene. "Who did you play with today?" I asked.

"Oh, everyone," she said airily.

"Oh," I said. Then Amantha proceeded to tell me how she had solved her problem.

What she had done, in fact, was exactly what Annie had done in the "stupid" story. Thus she had managed to take advice without losing her eleven-year-old sense of autonomy and dignity, a feat that greatly impressed me.

Another beneficial aspect of Annie Stories is that they provide a good old-fashioned dose of the loving intimacy of a bedtime story. This, in itself, is strengthening and comforting for both parent and child. In today's electronic world of TV and video games and the rush of juggling careers and parenting, the cozy comfort of storytelling time can be like the proverbial oasis in the desert.

Annie Stories are helpful for parents as well. There is nothing more distressing than watching our children suffer and feeling powerless to help them. Annie Stories provide parents with a simple and natural technique that really works. It empowers parents, and their increased confidence will be communicated to the child. Stories are a way of building a bridge between a frightened and perhaps uncommunicative child and a parent who wants to help but doesn't know how to get the message across.

Drawing, painting, and modeling with clay can be used in conjunction with Annie Stories, as children draw or model situations in the stories. Artwork provides a wonderful way for children to express and work through the things that are troubling them.

Often, for instance, children will draw a picture of the "monster" that has been bothering them, and then with obvious glee make a show of tearing up the picture. In doing this, they are symbolically tearing up the monster and demonstrating their mastery over it.

## Storytelling and Psychotherapy

The therapeutic value of storytelling for children is acknowledged by therapists of many different persuasions. It can be justified by such widely differing psychotherapeutic approaches as psychoanalysis and behavior therapy.

Psychoanalysts would talk about the beneficial aspects of the process of identification with the successful child in the story. They would acknowledge the cathartic effect of being able to recognize repressed feelings in a "safe" way through seeing them in the fictional alter ego.

Behavior therapists would see the stories as an effective way of utilizing social modeling techniques. The stories can also provide a particularly enjoyable way of teaching behavioral techniques such as desensitization, which is demonstrated in Chapter 8, Obsessive/Perfectionistic children.

Teachers have used the stories in classroom situations. As with the individual child, they provide a way for the class to discuss difficult subjects in a nonthreatening way.

Therapists have also used the stories as a means of communicating with children. After an Annie Stories workshop, one therapist told me about one of her patients. This child had been taken from a deprived home where she had been badly abused and placed in foster care. She had retreated into herself and was silent and uncommunicative. She remained so through several weeks of therapy until finally the therapist had the idea of telling her a story. The story was about a worm who lived in a rotten apple and had to find another home. The child seemed to come alive as she listened to the story. She was clearly fascinated by it. It was the first time she had shown an emotional response in therapy and it marked the beginning of a breakthrough in her relationship with her therapist.

Parent educators have also taught parents how to tell the stories. Here the technique has the value of being simple, effective, and easy to teach in a group setting.

For children whose problems seem particularly severe or do not resolve with time, consultation with a therapist is advisable. Long periods of depression, withdrawal, or aggressive acting-out may also be an indication that professional help is required. In addition, it is advisable to have your child checked out by a pediatrician or physician. Many symptoms of anxiety, such as dizziness, head-aches, and stomachaches, may be symptoms of physical illness, too. Yet even those children who need professional help can enjoy and benefit from Annie Stories.

# 2
# How to Use and Tell Annie Stories

Annie Stories are designed to be tailored to the needs of your particular child. Each child is an individual. The work of Thomas, Chess, and Birch as well as numerous other researchers has shown us that babies come with a variety of personal styles. Think about your child and her ways of coping with the world. For example, is she[1] cautious about trying out new experiences or does she charge right in? Is she adaptable to changes or do new routines make her fretful or anxious? How does she see herself? Does she think of herself as brave or timid, competent or clumsy, sociable or shy?

Begin by modeling Annie[2] on your child. Give her the same personality characteristics, the same ways of coping with anxiety, the same fears, and the same hopes. This similarity will help your child to identify with Annie and also, very importantly, to feel that when Annie succeeds, maybe she can, too.

For example, if your child is shy, a story about a shy child who moves to a new school and learns how to make friends will have more impact than a story about an outgoing, confident child. The outgoing, confident child may be seen as light years away from your child. Everyone "knows," after all, that outgoing, confident children find it easy to make friends. But if a shy child manages

---

[1]The feminine pronoun is used to refer to both girls and boys.
[2]I've used Annie as a name because it's similar to my daughter, Amantha's. You can pick a name for your heroine/hero that's similar to your child's.

to do it, that's different. Your child is able to think, "Well, if someone just like me can do it, then maybe I can do it, too."

Make Annie's problems and conflicts echo those of your child. This means they echo the way your child sees her problems, not necessarily the way you see them. Later on in the story, you can work up to Annie seeing her problems in a different light. At the beginning, the first thing to do is establish empathy and credibility. For instance, if your child is monumentally embarrassed because she is taller than everyone else in her class, she may well experience it as akin to being deformed. If you begin an Annie Story by saying, "Annie felt like the weirdest, ugliest person in the whole school," your child will think, "Yes, that's exactly the way I feel. She really knows what she's talking about." You can then go on to tell of how Annie ended up finding that her tallness was actually an asset, or that everyone else in the class also thought they were ugly, or whatever other resolution you choose to follow. Because you have begun by meeting your child where she is and showing her that you understand her feelings, she is much more likely to follow you through the coming shifts and changes as Annie learns to view her tallness in a different light.

If, however, you start by saying "Tallness is terrific," or "It's silly to worry about being tall," your child would have to defend her position. She would say or think, "Tallness is terrible. I hate being tall. I feel like a freak. You just don't understand at all." In defending herself, she would have closed herself off from what you are saying. Obviously she would be far less open to any further learning.

Keep things simple. Stick to concepts and language that your child will understand. Be aware of your child's attention span and tailor the length of your story to this.

The stories in this book are all quite long. I wanted to put in as many details as I could so that readers could pick out what was relevant to their particular children. The stories here are intended as guides—to provide information and ideas to help you make up your own stories. Many parents, however, are not yet confident enough of their own story-telling abilities and prefer to begin by reading these stories to their children. I've thus divided some stories into several parts. For children with shorter attention spans, you can read the stories in sections, spacing them over two or three days.

Remember to pick up your child's strengths in the stories as well as fears and conflicts. It's easy for children to lose perspective and forget that they have any strengths at all when they're mired in feelings of impotence and worthlessness.

Use humor whenever you can. Apart from engaging the child's interest, humor is a great antidote for tension and anxiety. When I told Amantha the first Annie Story about going to nursery school, I included a joke about a dog helicopter. Annie and her mom were watching Blackie, their dog, wag her tail. It was wagging so fast, they decided she would make a good helicopter. They made up a little fantasy about arriving at school via dog helicopter. In real life, I was walking Amantha to school on her very first day. As we started to walk through the gate, I could feel her hand tighten on mine as her anxiety rose. Suddenly she said, "Remember the dog helicopter?" We both started laughing, and she walked through the school gates laughing instead of tense.

Some stories involve helping the child learn to relax. For guidelines to this, use Chapter 14, Relaxation, in this book.

As you tell your Annie Story, watch your child for cues. Notice when she seems riveted, when the story seems to be going over her head, or when she seems bored. When she's riveted, you're clearly on the right track. If she's not interested in the story, you might be on the wrong track, or she might not be ready to hear this story yet.

If you're not sure where to go with your story line, ask your child—"What do you think Annie did next?" or "I wonder what Annie was thinking?" If your child says, "I don't know," play twenty questions with her. Guessing is an excellent way of finding out about things. Have her guess what Annie was thinking. If she contributes to the story, encourage her and take note of what she's saying. She is invariably telling you something important about herself.

Annie Stories should always end on a positive note. You need to give your child hope that she will be able to find a way out of her distress. A child who believes there is no hope has no motivation to continue the struggle. She will simply give up.

The way you achieve your positive ending will vary from story to story. It should be something your child can adapt and use. It may come from practical techniques such as desensitization (Chapter 6, Compulsive and Perfectionistic story) or social skills training (Chapter 7, Shyness story). It may come from the recognition, clarification, and validation of the child's feelings (some of the stories in Chapter 3 are examples of this). It may come from the knowledge that as time passes, an acutely felt sorrow can dim and become bearable.

The stories in the two volumes of Annie Stories will give you some idea of the variety of ways in which hope can triumph over sadness and fear. Your own life will give you more. Think back to occasions when you overcame distressing circumstances. We all have times, of course, when such circumstances overcome us, but at other times we have been healed after a wound or helped through a difficult experience. Sometimes, just the knowledge that we have been able to survive these experiences is a help in itself.

Remember that you don't have to be perfect. This is not a college essay that you're going to be graded on. Children are invariably helpful listeners. They'll assist you if you make a mistake. They'll correct you if you forget details. They'll let you know whether you're off track or on course. Instead of trying to be word perfect, relax into the story as much as you can. Let your imagination loose. Have fun with it.

It's important also to be aware of your own anxieties. If you are anxious while telling the story, your anxiety may be communicated to your child. In this situation, you might get another family member or friend who is more relaxed to tell the story. You can listen and pick up cues as to how she does it. Having a role model like this can help you feel more at ease when you tell a story.

Some parents who feel uncertain about their ability to make up stories prefer to start by reading the appropriate story, almost as it is, to their child. If you choose to do this, change the names and settings to ones that are suitable to your particular child. Read slowly and leave space for interjections by you and your child. After you've read the story a few times, and the plot is familiar to you, try telling it without the book. Your child will help you fill in any gaps, and you can also enjoy embroidering the details in your own way. The more you do it, the easier and more fun it gets.

I've set out below a step-by-step outline for making up your own Annie Stories:

1. Think about the problem that has created the need for a story. Try to tune in to how your child is feeling as he or she struggles with this problem. Try to see what the situation must look like from the child's perspective.
2. Think about the message of the story. What ideas do you want to get across to your child? What sort of solutions or resolutions would you like your story to suggest? The solutions don't have to be very complex. They can be based on some of the techniques taught in this book or they may be based on solutions you have found in your own life. These solutions may involve learning new practical or social skills, finding comfort through friends and family, learning that the passage of time can be healing, and so on.
3. Begin the story with a hero or heroine who mirrors your child's fears, anxieties, or conflicts. This allows your child to identify with the hero/heroine and draws the child into the story.
4. Give the hero/heroine some of the strengths and talents that your child possesses. Often when we're feeling anxious or overwhelmed by a problem, we forget that we have any strengths or talents. It's good to be reminded of them.
5. Start by allowing the plot to mirror the conflict in your child's life and then move on to its positive resolution.
6. Be open to your child as you tell the story. Notice when the child seems engrossed or when he or she seems impatient. You'll get clues as to where the story is hitting home from your child's expression.
7. If your child makes comments or asks questions about the stories, be responsive to these. They will often give you valuable insights into your child's thinking. If you have trouble answer-

ing the questions, you can turn them back to the child with a "What do you think?" If the child says "I don't know," you can make a guessing game out of it. Children's guesses in this sort of situation usually give good clues as to what they're thinking.

8. If you don't know why your child is feeling worried in a particular situation, you can use the Annie Story to explore this. As you tell the Annie Story, intersperse it with comments such as "And what do you think Annie was worried about then?" or "What was Annie scared of?" or "What did Annie think would happen?" and so on.

9. If your child tries out a solution you have suggested in a previous Annie Story and it doesn't work, don't panic. Find out exactly what she did and what went wrong. Then tell an Annie Story about a little girl who did what she did, found to her dismay that it didn't work, but persevered and found something that did. However, it may be that you really haven't a clue as to why the technique used in the story failed. In that case, an Annie Story in which Annie is disappointed about her failure but nevertheless resolves to find a way out of her dilemma may be appropriate. You can also focus on the fact that Annie and her family felt very proud of her for trying, even though her efforts failed.

10. Keep it simple. Gear the vocabulary to your child's level and the length to your child's attention span.

11. You and your story don't have to be perfect. Ignore your fumbles and if you become aware of any goofs (often from your child's expression), simply correct them with an "Oops, I almost forgot, she didn't go by herself, she went with a friend," or whatever the mistake relates to. Often your child will correct you with a pitying glance that says, "Poor Mom, can't even remember a story right." This doesn't seem to dim either her enjoyment or her use of the story, and neither should it dim yours.

# 3

# How to Teach Annie Stories

I am often asked about the best way to teach Annie Stories. The books of course provide a way of learning and trying out the storytelling technique. Another way of learning how to tell and use Annie Stories is through the hands-on experience of a workshop.

For someone who is new to the storytelling technique, the two foremost questions are likely to be "Can *I* tell stories?" and "What's the point of telling stories?"

A workshop allows people to get in touch with their own ability to make up and tell stories. It also allows them to explore the impact of storytelling, both in terms of the stories they tell and the story that is told to them.

Workshops can be structured to run for a full day or for a few hours. A full day is the ideal time because it gives everyone a chance to tell a story and to have one told to them. However, even the shorter workshops give participants the chance to experience stories in action. They are ideal ways for groups of therapists, teachers, parent educators, or parents to learn the storytelling technique.

The workshop starts off with a brief exposition of the value of stories and how they work and then moves into the experiential side of things.

People divide up into groups of three. Within these small groups, each member thinks of something that was a problem for him or her as a child. If participants don't wish to use their own experiences, they can use those of a child patient or a child they know. They describe this problem to the other members of the

21

group in as much detail as they can and from a child's-eye perspective. They describe how they felt about the problem, how they tried to solve it, how they ended up coping or not coping, how the people around them reacted to it. All this is conveyed in terms of how they experienced it in childhood, not how they now see it from an adult viewpoint.

At this point in the workshop, there is a noticeable change in the atmosphere. What has started off as a room full of colleagues with a very work-a-day air suddenly shifts. The atmosphere warms and softens. All around the room, you hear a buzz of comments such as, "I felt like that, too," "I remember that," "Me, too," as people recognize the universality of many childhood experiences. Groups are engrossed in conversation and memories as they are transported back to childhood.

The problems worked on by the groups don't have to be large, serious, or intense problems. In a workshop setting, it is more appropriate that problems are smaller, but nevertheless real ones for that particular child. To give an example of some of the diverse problems that have been brought up in workshops:

One boy was bright at all of his schoolwork except math. He hated working with numbers and felt inadequate and angry during math classes. One girl was riding a horse when it bolted. She had felt uneasy around horses ever since. One boy dreaded his aunts' visits. They always insisted on greeting him with a kiss on the cheek. He hated being kissed but got into trouble with his parents for being impolite if he tried to wriggle away from them. One boy, a patient, had suffered facial burns in an accident and was mortified by the fact that his scars made him look different from the other kids.

Having heard the problem, people now focus on what would have helped this particular child feel better. How could this problem have been resolved? What interventions might have made a difference? The group goes through each of the problems that has been brought up, focusing on what would have helped this particular child at this particular time. The solutions or resolutions the group comes up with will eventually be incorporated into an Annie Story.

The small groups then reform into the large group. This is a time for feedback. Any problems that a small group feels stymied by can be brought to the large group for a brainstorming session.

For the next section of the workshop, participants move back into their small groups of three. Two members of each group go off together to make up the Annie Story. They then return to tell it to the third member of the group. This process continues until each member of the group has listened to a story and has in turn told a story.

Working in groups of three means that no one has to make up a story on his or her own. There is always someone to toss ideas around with. If the small group gets stuck, there is the large group to turn to. One idea sparks off another idea. People who thought they could never make up stories find themselves weaving quite intricate tales with increasing delight and ease. It is as if the group atmosphere offers an opportunity to safely loosen up and get in touch with our imagination.

For the listener, the recipient of the story, there is the experience of discovering the special nourishment inherent in a story told just for you. Participants who have started off the workshop feeling cynical about stories have ended up describing how surprisingly moved they felt as their stories were told to them. Many have found themselves remembering feelings they had forgotten even when initially describing the problem to the group. People comment on how comforted and validated they feel as they listen to their story. Many describe experiencing a feeling of "closure" about an episode that had remained unfinished but in the background for a long time.

One participant in a workshop, whom I shall refer to as Kate, described a childhood incident which she felt had had a great impact on her. The incident, although relatively innocuous, resulted in her feeling tremendously embarrassed and foolish. Kate spent a lot of time from then on avoiding situations in which she might feel embarrassed or foolish. She was aware, however, that in doing so she was restricting her potential to learn and grow.

The story we told Kate was about a little girl called Cathy who had done something really embarrassing. She had felt stupid and humiliated. She was sure that no one else could have done such a stupid thing.

One day Cathy's grade was organizing a charity concert. Everyone had to think of a way to raise money. Some people were doing singing and dancing acts. Some people were baking cookies to sell during the intermission. Cathy didn't want to do any of those things. She didn't know what she could do. She thought and thought. Suddenly, she had an idea. She would organize a competition called "The Stupidest Thing I Ever Did." Kids would pay to put in an entry describing the stupidest thing they had ever done. Cathy and some of her friends would read the entries on stage and the one who got the most audience applause would win a prize. When the entries came in, Cathy laughed and laughed over them. She hadn't realized that so many people could do such dumb things. It was a good feeling. She wrote her own entry, too. She really wanted it to win, but with all the other great entries, she wasn't sure that it would.

When the big day came, Cathy and her friends read out the entries. The audience clapped and howled and roared with laughter. They loved it. And guess whose entry they loved best. Yes, it was Cathy's. Cathy couldn't stop smiling. People crowded around her and told her how terrific she'd been, what a great idea it was, how much money she'd raised, and what a good time they'd had. People kept coming up and telling her about still more stupid things they'd done. They asked her if she'd organize the same event for next year so that they could enter it, too. Cathy smiled and smiled. In fact, she couldn't stop smiling.

Kate, who had this Cathy Story told to her, wrote me a letter after the workshop describing the experience.

*Dear Doris,*

*I would like to tell you a story.*

*There was a girl called Kate. Kate had a big secret that she carried around with her. Sometimes the weight of the secret stopped her from doing all the wonderful things that Kate wanted to do. The secret was that Kate was a big fraud. She wasn't what she seemed to people. She wasn't like everybody else. She had a chink in herself: an embarrassment chink. She had had this chink for a long time, since she was six.*

*The embarrassment chink stopped Kate from doing a lot of the things that she wanted to do. Somehow Kate thought that if she did the things she wanted to do, really really well, and then people saw her chink, something disastrous would happen. So Kate just did things to the level she thought would be safe: not too well to become really famous and then to be found out, and not too badly to draw attention to herself. She didn't want people to find the chink.*

*What happened when Kate started doing the things she liked doing, better than the safe level, was that the chink opened up and Kate poured lots and lots of embarrassment into it, so that it grew. It went from being a small little hole to being an enormous one— almost bigger than Kate herself. Then she would stop doing the things she liked doing, better than the safe level she set, and feel all empty and failed inside.*

*One day Kate met Doris. Doris told stories and all the people around Kate also started telling stories. Kate found herself telling a story. It was the one about how she had first got her embarrassment chink. This was a big painful memory. But suddenly something magical happened. The people told it back to her and gave her some special salve, which they poured into her chink. Suddenly the chink started to change. It started to heal from the inside out. Soon all that was left of Kate's chink was a tiny fine line. She couldn't stop smiling.*

*Then the people around her who had given her the salve showed her that they all had tiny little lines, too, where their chinks had healed.*

*Kate suddenly stopped feeling a fraud. She felt normal. She knew she could go and do all the things she wanted to do, and reach as high as she wanted to. She was part of the human race.*

*Doris, I am still smiling. I have had a wonderful day.*
*Thank you very much.*

Another participant, Rosemary, described an incident which had happened when she was eight. She had been walking to the store on an errand for her mother. Before crossing the road, she looked to the left and then to the right (this was an Australian workshop—we drive on the wrong side of the road!) as she had been taught. There was a car coming but Rosemary judged that she could cross the road safely. She ran across the road, but the car was coming faster than she had thought. It had to screech to a stop to avoid her. Rosemary stood on the other side of the road shaking and shivering with fright. The woman driver got out of her car and started shrieking at Rosemary. She called her an idiot, a bad girl, and a hopeless child. The local shopkeeper, attracted by the noise, also came out and started screaming at Rosemary. Rosemary was petrified. She felt horribly ashamed and guilty. She was too scared to tell her parents what had happened in case they thought she was terrible, too. She was terrified that the driver would track her down and tell her parents. When she walked along the sidewalk, she would turn her head away from passing cars so that if the woman was in one, she wouldn't see her. When she was being driven in the car, she would bob down every time a car passed by.

Rosemary's group told her a story about a little girl who was crossing the road when she was nearly run over by a car. The woman driver of the car got out and screamed at her. The little girl was scared, but she realized that the woman was an evil witch whom people had been trying to catch for a long time. The little girl knew that next time she crossed the road, she should be more cautious, but she knew she didn't deserve to get screamed at like that. The little girl kept an eye out for the witch and when she spotted her again, she was able to help people capture her. The little girl became a heroine. Everyone wanted to see the girl who had captured a witch. When she went for a drive, people would wave at her, and she would sit in the car and wave back. When she went for a walk, people in cars would wave and cheer when they saw her. She felt terrific.

Rosemary talked to me some time after the workshop. She said that the story had had quite an impact on her. She said, "I enjoyed listening to the story and felt a sense of relief at the end of it. I realized that I had felt so guilty, I had never allowed myself to feel angry at the woman for the way she had treated me. It was such a relief to feel angry. I also realized that she had probably been upset at the time she lashed out at me. It seems so simple to realize that now, but it had just never occurred to me. I caught the train home after the workshop. Sitting on the train, I felt very light with a real sense of well-being. When I got off the train, I had to walk along a fairly narrow sidewalk with a lot of cars driving past. That was when I really noticed the difference. I felt as if I were walking on air. I was walking so tall it felt as if my feet were barely touching the ground. All around me the colors seemed much richer. The sky seemed bluer. It had been raining and the scents of the grass and flowers seemed incredibly sweet. It was a wonderful feeling."

During the workshop, participants also experience the importance of listening and of trying to empathically understand and enter into the child's world.

As an example, I'll take one of the problems previously mentioned, that of the girl whose horse had bolted. The woman to whom this had happened described the incident to her workshop group and mentioned that she had been uneasy around horses ever since. On the surface it seemed like a classic case of phobic anxiety. Girl gets scared when her horse bolts and thereafter is anxious with horses. However, as the participant told her story and her fellow group members questioned her, a somewhat different theme emerged. What the young girl had found most upsetting about the incident did not have to do with fears for her safety. What had been most upsetting for her had been her conviction that she should have been able to control the horse. She felt that it was her fault that the horse had bolted. She felt inadequate and ashamed. She believed that this incident showed that she was incompetent.

The story we made up for her was very simple. It was a story about a girl whose horse had bolted. It wasn't her fault, horses do sometimes get frightened and bolt. When the horse finally drew up, with her clinging desperately to it, there was a crowd of onlookers. They rushed forward.

"Wow!" said one. "How on earth did you manage to stay in the saddle? That was really impressive."

"That was an amazing ride," said another. "You were terrific."

"Boy," said another one, "I would have been thrown after the first minute. How did you do it?"

The comments continued in this vein. The listener's face as she was told this story was wreathed in smiles.

Making up stories also allows you to get in touch with your sense of fun and playfulness. Take, for example, a problem mentioned previously—that of the boy who didn't like math. This boy grew up to be a man who had graduated from college and done well in all his studies, but who still hated numbers. As he talked with his group, he recalled how humiliated he had felt by his experiences with math and how angry and resentful he had been when called upon to work with figures.

The story we told him was about a little boy who hated numbers. He thought he couldn't do them and he would get very angry at them. He felt as if they were just there to trick him and trip him up. He didn't want to have anything to do with numbers. So you can imagine that he was not very happy when one day the teacher asked him to come out in front of the class and solve the equation on the blackboard. He came and stood in front of the blackboard and glared at the numbers on it.

"Huh," he said to them, "you think you're pretty smart, don't you." He felt like taking the eraser and wiping them all off. In fact, he felt like wiping off all the numbers all over the world. He glared at them some more. Then, all of a sudden, something very strange happened. The numbers fell off the blackboard. One minute they were sitting on the blackboard, the next minute they were squirming helplessly on the floor. The boy was startled. He bent down to have a closer look at them. They were wriggling around on their backs like funny little beetles, desperately trying to right themselves. They saw him looking at them.

"Help!" they squealed. "Please help us."

The boy bent down closer. They looked very pathetic.

"Please," they said to him, "you're the only one who can help us. Please, would you put us back on the board? We're all mixed up and confused. We need you to tell us where to go."

"Oh," said the boy. He was beginning to feel quite sorry for them. "How will I know what order to put you in?"

The numbers got quite excited. They jiggled up and down. "You mean you'll help us?" they said. "Oh, wow! This is great. You know, we used to feel so awful when you hated us."

"Really?" the boy said. He was amazed.

"Yes," said the numbers. "Sometimes we even used to cry when you ignored us."

"But you never heard us," said another number. "And we couldn't figure out how to get you to hear us."

"Gee," said the boy. "That's really weird. I used to think you didn't want anything to do with me."

"But of course we did," said the numbers. "Numbers can't do anything on their own. We need someone like you to help us do what we're supposed to do."

"Oh," said the boy. "You mean you really wanted to be friends with me?"

"We sure did," said the numbers. "We've been wanting to be friends with you for ages. We have loads of good games that we could play together."

"Golly," said the boy. He was beginning to feel quite excited. "Maybe we could do that."

"Okay," said the numbers. "Why don't you start by helping us back up on the board. Then we can all figure out where we belong."

The little boy got quite friendly with the numbers after that. They taught him lots of number games. In fact, he used to like playing with the numbers so much that he often forgot to come down for dinner. His mother got quite irritated with him.

"Albert!" she used to call. "It's dinner time."

When he still didn't come, because he was busy finishing off a number game, she got even more irritated.

"Albert!" she would say, standing in the corridor with her hands on her hips. "Albert Einstein, when are you going to come down for dinner!"

Another amusing solution was invented for the boy who hated to be kissed by his aunts. What he really hated about the situation was his powerlessness. He felt that his needs were being ignored. He had tried asserting himself about this issue, but it had only resulted in punishment. In the story we made up for him, the little boy had a wonderful idea. He got a jar and poured into it a mixture of the most horrible substances he could think of. These included foul potions such as the water that broccoli had been boiled in, a touch of the tooth paste he hated, and so on. When his aunts arrived at the door, he would go to his jar, dip a finger in it, and dab it on his cheek on the exact spot that his aunts always kissed. Then he would go downstairs, smiling at his secret, knowing that when his aunts kissed him, they would be kissing broccoli water. He loved it. He felt autonomous and back in control again.

For the boy who was troubled by his facial scars, we made up a story about the knights of old. The boldest and bravest of these knights used to visit this little boy at night and tell him stories about great and chivalrous adventures. He explained to the little boy about how, in those days, knights went about fighting for right and defeating evil-doers. The knight who was able to right the most wrongs was revered and held up as the standard for all the others to aspire to. It was easy to tell who this knight was. Because he had been in the most battles against evil, he was the one who carried the most marks of these battles—his scars. His scars were a badge of honor and everyone who saw them knew how brave and gallant he must have been.

The story settings can range from everyday realism to the once-upon-a-time land of witches and wizards. As long as the problems parallel those of the child, the stories can be set anywhere and peopled with anything from ordinary children to wizards and talking animals. The two workshop stories outlined below provide examples of an everyday setting and a magical setting.

One workshop participant's father had been harshly perfectionistic. He had set excessively high standards for his daughter, and nothing she ever did was good enough. She had wanted to tell her father how she felt about this but had not been able to.

The story we made up for her involved a little girl who could never do anything well enough to please her father. She wanted to tell her father how she felt about this but she was too scared. She thought and thought about how to do it and finally came up with an idea. She would write a story about a little boy who felt just as she did and who had a father just like hers. When her father read the story, he would realize how she felt. So she got her pen and paper and wrote out her story.

Very nervously, she gave the story to her father to read. To her amazement, her father's expression changed as he read the story. He began to look quite sad. "Goodness," he said when he'd finished reading, "that boy sounds just like I was with my father when I was little." The girl was amazed. "You mean you felt that way about your dad?" she said. Her father nodded. "Yes," he said, remembering, "it was awful."

Suddenly he looked at the little girl. "Do you feel like that about me?" he asked. The little girl nodded her head yes. "Oh," said her father, looking very thoughtful. "You know, I hadn't realized it was like that. Maybe we should talk about this." The little girl nodded her head again. "I'd like that," she said.

Another participant in a workshop wanted a story for a patient of hers. The patient was the school-refusing daughter of an agoraphobic mother. Because of the child's school refusal and the mother's agoraphobia, the pair stayed indoors most of the time. The story we made up concerned a queen and a princess who lived in a faraway land. The queen and princess stayed inside the castle all the time because a wizard had put a spell on them. The wizard had told them that if they went outside, something terrible would happen. The princess and her mother were frightened and decided that it would be safer never to go out.

At first that worked out okay, but then, inside the castle, things started to get difficult. The princess noticed it first. She noticed that she and her mother were getting smaller. The longer they stayed in the castle without going out, the smaller they got. At first it was just an inconvenience, having to stretch up to cupboards, shoes that got too big, and so on. But as they got smaller and smaller, every day became more and more of a trial, and there were more and more things they couldn't do.

The Princess began to think that maybe staying inside all the time wasn't such a good idea. But what would happen to her if she went outside? She was worrying about this when there was a knock on the door. It was the postman bringing their mail.

You're looking worried, Princess," he said. So the princess told him all about her problem. "Oh my goodness!" he said when she had finished. "I know that wizard and he's a big fake. His spells never ever work. I'm sure nothing at all would happen to you if you went outside."

"Really?" said the Princess. She thought for a while about what it would be like to go outside. "But I haven't been outside in a long time," she explained to the postman. "I might not know what to do."

"There are a lot of people who know you outside," said the postman, "and you know them from the time before the spell. You could always ask them for help and they would be happy to give it to you."

The princess thought about what the postman had said. She decided to try going outside. She was a bit nervous as she opened the castle door and crossed over the moat. But the postman was right. The wizard's spell didn't work. Nothing bad happened at all. The princess went outside regularly. She noticed that each time she went outside, she got bigger and stronger. Soon she was back to her normal size and could do all the things that she used to be able to do. She felt very pleased with herself.

This story can be expanded and shaped in different ways in response to the needs of the child. It could, for instance, explore what it felt like for the princess when she realized that the queen was also under the wizard's spell and couldn't be turned to for help. Or it could focus on the princess's experience at Princess School, and how she learned to handle that.

The group decided to focus on this particular aspect of the story because it was designed to be shared with the child's mother. They felt that the experience of being too scared to venture out into the big world was a theme that would resonate for both mother and daughter. This illustrates another way in which therapists can use the stories—to help parents get in touch with their child's world, and perhaps their own, and to assist them in spending this special time with their children.

It's helpful, too, to remember that the stories don't have to cover everything all at once. They can deal with different aspects of the problem at different times.

A good example is Rosemary's story, which was described a few pages earlier. She was the little girl who was nearly knocked over by a car. Rosemary's group felt that the most pressing and disturbing aspect of Rosemary's near-accident was the fact that it left her feeling like a hunted criminal. They decided to focus on this and used the story to reverse the situation. Rosemary was certainly aware that she had been too hasty in crossing the road—she didn't need this emphasized to her—but she was feeling a burden of shame and guilt that went far beyond what the situation called for. Her group could also have created a story explaining that the driver was yelling so much because she herself was scared. Interestingly, this follow-up wasn't necessary because, freed from the excessive guilt, Rosemary was able to realize this for herself.

The stories described here illustrate just some of the ways in which therapeutic stories can be woven from the fabric of pain and distress. That, too, is one of the pleasures of a workshop—getting to hear so many stories enriches the treasure trove in which you will find your own.

# 4

# *Fear of the Dark*

Fear of the dark is one of the most common fears in children. It often starts around three years of age and extends through the pre-teen years and beyond.

For most of us, darkness is disorienting. All of the familiar land-marks of our daytime lives have disappeared. Even if they have not disappeared, they have been radically altered in appearance, seeming more sinister and mysterious than their daylight coun-terparts. The dark is a place of shadows and ambiguity. It is also the time when we feel most isolated and alone with our thoughts, our fantasies, and our fears.

For most children, fear of the dark is related to what might be lurking in the dark. Sometimes, however, this fear generalizes to the state of darkness itself and becomes a phobic fear of the dark. This type of fear can be treated along the lines of other sorts of pho-bic fears. The procedure and an appropriate story for phobic fears has been set out in the first Annie Stories book (Fear of Dogs).

For the purposes of this chapter, I am assuming that the child's fear of the dark is focused on the monsters she sees in its shadows.

The experience of seeing monsters in the dark is so common as to be almost universal. Young children, who invariably possess rich imaginative powers, are unable to distinguish fantasy from reality. To them, the monsters they see are as real as you or I. It is very common for parents to reassure frightened children by say-ing that there are no such things as monsters, witches, or whatever nasty characters their children may have conjured up. Children just don't believe you. They may accept that there are no monsters in their room right now, while you are in it, but they know per-fectly well that as soon as you leave and turn out the lights, the monsters will reappear.

Furthermore, telling them that monsters don't exist and they are just being silly makes them feel belittled and misunderstood. Frightened children feel inadequate enough without this extra stress. It is certainly useful to turn the light on, point out to the child that the vicious creature she saw was actually a bundle of clothes on the chair, and so on. But it is also important to give children a means of coping with monsters when you are not there in the room. In other words, it is important to help them feel stronger and less at the mercy of their monsters.

Monsters are often the projection of a child's angry feelings or fears. They contain the "bad" feelings that the child finds difficult to deal with. Thus, in allowing the child to explore and stand up to her monsters, you are also allowing her to feel more comfortable with her feelings and less frightened of them. In effect, in mastering her monsters, she is reclaiming and mastering aspects of herself.

Sometimes, children's night fears center around burglars or kidnappers. This may be especially true if there have been such events discussed on the news or in the neighborhood. For children who are scared of robbers, kidnappers, etc., it is useful to go through with them the practical steps they could take if, for instance, they heard a burglar. For example, they might run into their parents' room or call out loudly. Show your children that there are locks on the doors and windows, and that they are kept secured at night. Children can also construct their own alarm systems or burglar deterrents. These can be quite imaginative. They are usually totally useless against a real burglar but extremely comforting for the child. They act as a sort of "magic" solution, allowing the child to feel in control again.

It is also important to make the bedroom a comforting place for children to be. Don't use sending them to bed as a punishment or they may come to associate this room with bad feelings. A room associated with bad feelings provides a monster-friendly environment.

Invest in a night light for your child that she is able to turn up or down at will. A "magic" anti-monster device such as the one used in the following Annie Story is extremely helpful. It can be anything from a magic flashlight to an empty aerosol can.

It can also be helpful for your child to draw the monsters and then tear them up or model them in clay and squash them. This allows your child not only to express her "monstrous" feelings but also to become less frightened of them and gain mastery over them.

## annie story

Annie was a little girl who lived in a brown brick house with her mommy and her daddy and a big black dog.[1]

It was getting near bedtime in Annie's house. Annie's bedtime, that is. Annie was desperately trying to think of things she could do to put off going to bed.[2]

"I'm very hungry," she announced to her mom. "I think I'll have to have a big meal before going to bed."

"No, you won't, darling," said her mom. "You had a perfectly good dinner. It's too late to be eating right now."

Annie thought for a minute. "There's a TV show I want to watch. I'll have to stay up for it."

"No, you won't," said her mom. "Bedtime is in five minutes."

"I forgot to tell Nancy something," said Annie. "I'll have to phone her and tell her now."

"Nancy will be asleep, sweetheart," said her mom. "You can tell her at school tomorrow."

"I have to have a glass of water," said Annie.

"You had one just a minute ago," said her mom. "I think it's time to go to bed now."

Annie's mom gave her a kiss as she tucked her in. "Goodnight, sleep tight, don't let the bedbugs bite," she said.

Annie groaned. It wasn't the bedbugs she was worried about. It was the other things. Still, maybe she would be lucky. Maybe they wouldn't come tonight.

---

[1] Vary the details here to suit your child's environment.

[2] Children who are scared of monsters in the dark often go through all sorts of contortions in order to delay bedtime.

Her mom switched off the light. Annie could hear her footsteps echoing down the hall. She felt very alone and very afraid. She tunneled under the covers as if she were a little worm scrambling away from the early bird.

She felt safer under the covers. No one could see her and she couldn't see anyone. It was like being invisible. Annie thought you could have great fun being invisible. You could sneak up to someone and yell "Boo!" in their ear just as they were about to pour syrup onto their pancakes. You could listen in and hear what your mom and dad were talking about when they kept their voices low and made you play in the other room. You could creep into nasty Jenny Brown's house at night and make ghost noises at her. That would show her that she shouldn't be mean to Annie at school.

Annie sighed. The trouble with being invisible under the blanket, though, was that it got very hot. The other trouble was that as soon as you poked your nose out from under the blanket, you became visible again. So it wasn't really very useful. Still, maybe she would be lucky tonight and they wouldn't be there at all.

Slowly, very slowly, Annie wriggled out from under the covers. She opened her eyes and looked around. The room was very dark. She could see the cupboards. She could see the curtains and the faint glow of the street lights through the window. She could see her desk. She could see . . .

"Aaagh!" She leaped out of bed and ran screaming into the living room.

Her mother jumped up. "Annie!" she said. "Annie, darling, what's wrong?"

"It's the monsters," said Annie. "There are monsters in my room." And she started to cry.

Annie's mom hugged her tight. "You look as if they gave you a big scare," she said.

Annie nodded. "They were big, mean monsters," she said. "They were trying to get me."

"Would you like me to come back to your room with you?" asked Annie's mom.

Annie nodded.

"But first," her mom continued, "I want to get something from the kitchen. I have something there that monsters are terrified of."

"Really?" said Annie.

"Definitely," said her mom. "Monsters absolutely cannot stand this thing. They run away as soon as they see it."

"What is it?" asked Annie. She was getting excited. Imagine her mom having a monster weapon in the kitchen!

When they got to the kitchen, Annie's mom opened a drawer and took out something. It was like a short, thick, plastic stick with glass at one end. It was a shiny blue color.

Annie stared at it doubtfully.

"This," said her mom, "is a special, magic, monster light.[3] Look." She flicked a switch on the side of the flashlight.

"Oh," said Annie, looking at the beam of light that spread from the flashlight. "But how does it work?"

"Well," said her mom, "monsters are afraid of the light."

"Really?" said Annie.

"Really," said her mom. "You know how you're afraid of the dark? Well, monsters are afraid of the light."

"Hey," said Annie. She was beginning to get the picture. "So you mean that whenever I see monsters when I'm lying in the dark, all I need to do is switch on the magic monster light and they'll run away?"

"That's right," said her mom. "They especially can't stand the beam from the magic monster light." She took Annie's hand. "Come on, we'll go to your room and turn on the light and you'll see that there are no monsters there."

When they got to her room, Annie looked all around very carefully. She looked in the cupboard, behind the curtain, and under the bed, but she couldn't find a single monster.

"It's true," said Annie. "The light must have scared them away."

"Now," said her mom, "you can snuggle into your bed quite safely, and we can put your magic monster light right here next to your bed."

---

[3]I've used a flashlight here, but other objects such as an empty aerosol spray can, for instance, would also be suitable.

"Good," said Annie. She felt safe with her magic monster light near her.

"Night, night," said her mom and gave her a kiss.

Annie closed her eyes and went straight off to sleep.[4]

The next morning, Annie asked, "Can I have some cardboard and a big black marker?"

"Sure," said her mom. "What would you like it for?"

"It's a secret," said Annie. "I'll show it to you when I've finished it."

She went into her room and started working.

An hour later, she came out. "Look what I've made," she said to her mom, and she held up a big cardboard sign.

"MONSTERS KEEP OUT," it said. "THIS ROOM IS PROTECTED BY THE MAGIC MONSTER LIGHT."[5]

"Wow," said Annie's mom, "that should certainly scare the monsters off."

Annie nodded proudly.

"What did your monsters look like?" asked Annie's mom.

"They were mean and nasty," said Annie.

"Why don't you do a drawing of them?" said Annie's mom. "Then you can show me how mean and nasty they looked."[6]

"Okay," said Annie. She liked doing drawings. She drew the monsters just as she had seen them the other night. She made their eyes glow-in-the-dark yellow and gave them sharp pointy teeth with bright red tongues.

"My goodness," said Annie's mom, "they do look vicious." She took a closer look at them. "They look angry, too."

"They were very angry," said Annie. "They were even angrier than I was when Jenny said mean things about me to Sarah and then I fell over on my bike and then you wouldn't let me stay up late to watch TV." She paused for breath. "And that happened all on the same day."

---

[4]This is the end of the first part of the story. You can take a break here.

[5]Activities like this can help the child feel more in control.

[6]Artwork helps the child express her feelings about the monsters and can also help give her a sense of mastery over them.

"All on the same day," said Annie's mom. "That must have been a very miserable, angry day for you."

"It sure was," said Annie.

"Did you know," said Annie's mom, "that sometimes when you've been feeling very angry and you don't know what to do with it, your anger sneaks out at night and disguises itself so that it looks like monsters?"

"Really?" said Annie. Her eyes were wide open with surprise. Her mom nodded.

"Why would it do that?" asked Annie.

"Perhaps because it wants to get noticed," said her mom. "Sometimes because it has something to tell you."

"Can anger hurt anyone?" asked Annie.

"No," said her mom. "Anger is just a feeling. It's like a sort of energy. When too much of it builds up, it needs to be let out. Like when a kettle boils, the steam has to get out. To let out anger energy, you could do things like punch a pillow or stamp up and down on the sidewalk or do a painting about anger."[7]

"Are all my monsters made of my anger?" asked Annie.

"Well, a lot are probably made of anger," said her mom. "Some might be made of other sorts of feelings such as when you're sad or frightened, for instance, and some might not even know what they're made of. But they usually all have something they can tell you if you just get to talk to them. Sometimes you can even make friends with them. Sometimes you can tell them that they look silly. That embarrasses them, and monsters hate being embarrassed. They all have something that they're worried about. Some think their ears are too big or that their nose is too red. Sometimes they end up getting scared of you. They may look very fierce and vicious but they aren't nearly as tough as they look."[8] Annie's mom paused. "And, of course, you have your magic monster light now, so they're going to be terrified of you."

"Yes," said Annie. "I like my magic monster light."

---

[7]For more on anger, see Chapter 6 on Compulsive and Perfectionist Children.

[8]This allows the child to see her monsters in a different light. Some of the ideas in the Annie Story on nightmares (in the first book) can also be applied to monsters.

A few nights later, Annie was lying in bed. It was dark and she was just getting ready to doze off when all of a sudden she saw something. She opened her eyes wide and looked harder. There it was, over in the corner of her room, a MONSTER.

Annie grabbed her special magic monster light and switched it on.

The monster jumped. "No!" it squealed. It was very strange to see such a big ferocious monster making such a pathetic sound. "Not the magic monster light!" it squealed, backing away. "Not the flashlight! Anything but that! Please, turn it off."

"The flashlight stays on," said Annie firmly. "At least until you go."[9]

"It's not fair," said the monster. "You're supposed to be scared of me." It stamped one foot. "It's not fair," it said again. "What am I going to do?" Then it gave a big sniff, lifted one paw up to its face, and rubbed its eyes.

To her surprise, Annie saw that it was crying.[10]

"Are you all right?" she asked.

"What a stupid question," said the monster crossly. "Of course, I'm all right. I've just been shined at by a big horrible magic monster light, given a great big shock, and then found that you're not even frightened of me. What makes you think I wouldn't be all right?" And the monster stared defiantly at Annie. "I've never felt better in my whole life," it said and gave a great big sob.

"Oh," said Annie. She thought for a few moments. Then she said, "I think I know what your problem is. Or at least one of your problems."

"One of my many problems," said the monster grouchily. "All right, smartypants, what is it? What's my problem?"

"You're angry," said Annie. "That's your problem."

"Of course, I'm angry," said the monster. "But that's not my

---

[9]The roles are now reversed—Annie is the boss and the monster is subservient.

[10]The more pathetic the monster looks, the stronger and more in control the child can feel.

problem. My problem is that when I'm angry I like to go out and frighten people. That's what we were taught to do in monster school. And that's what I've always done. My problem is that this time you won't frighten."

"You mean I won't *be* frightened," said Annie.

The monster gave another sob. "And you're even correcting my grammar," it said. It was beginning to cry loudly now.

Annie felt concerned. "Don't cry," she said. "I think I have the answer."

The monster sniffed and looked up.

"My mom taught me a much better thing to do when you're angry," she said.

The monster gave another sniff. "Well?" it said cautiously.

"Come over here and I'll tell you about it," said Annie.

The monster pointed worriedly at the flashlight. "Not with that thing on, I won't," it said.

"Okay," said Annie and she switched it off. "Is that better?"

The monster nodded.

"Well, then," said Annie, and she patted the bed very gently because she didn't want to frighten the monster again, "come and sit over here."[11]

So the monster came and sat on Annie's bed, while Annie told it all about what to do with anger.

"Hey," said the monster, "that sounds pretty neat."

Annie nodded, pleased.

"Do you think," said the monster, "that you could help me try it out? I like the idea of punching the anger out into a pillow."

"Okay," said Annie. "Why not? Look, we can use my pillow here."

"Great," said the monster. And they both started pounding Annie's pillow.

"Hey," said Annie, "this is fun."

"This is a great idea," said the monster.

---

[11]Annie has now become the monster's protector and teacher as she befriends it—a real turn-around from the situation at the beginning of the story.

"I've got a better idea," squeaked the pillow. "Why don't you pound the mattress?"

But neither Annie nor the monster heard it because they were too busy rolling around in fits of laughter.

# 5

## Bedwetting

Bedwetting is the desperately kept secret of over five million children in the USA. Each one of them is quietly convinced that he or she is the only one in the world with such a terrible, curl-your-toes-up-and-die, embarrassing problem.

Studies have shown that approximately 10% of six-year-old children wet their beds at night, with boys 50% more likely to wet their beds than girls. Each year, approximately 15% of them will spontaneously stop wetting. Of the rest of these children, a great many will be feeling miserable and frustrated as they wake each morning to a urine-soaked bed.

Occasionally, bedwetting may be caused by a medical problem such as a urinary tract infection or diabetes, but for most children it is simply due to a maturational lag. Seventy percent of bedwetting children have a close relative who was also a bedwetter.

Most bedwetting is called "primary" bedwetting, where the child has never had an extended period of dryness at night. "Secondary" bedwetting occurs when a child who has been dry for a while begins to wet the bed again. Sometimes this is associated with stress. For instance, when a new baby arrives, the older child may regress to wetting the bed.

The most common causes of bedwetting are a bladder that hasn't learned to hold enough urine or an irritable bladder. The bladder that hasn't learned to hold enough urine is usually capable of holding much more. When it is only partially full, however, it gives off signals (bladder contractions) that give its owner the sense of needing to empty it urgently.

The amount of urine that a bladder can hold before sending "Empty me" signals is called its "functional capacity."

The aim of the program outlined in this Annie Story is to train the bladder to hold more urine, increase the child's awareness of bladder signals so that she doesn't sleep through them, and increase the tone of the muscles that control the opening and closing of the bladder.

Children often become very demoralized by their bedwetting. They feel ashamed, inadequate, and out of control. Don't add to this by scolding or belittling them. The more incompetent they feel, the less likely they are to take up the challenge and succeed in keeping their beds dry.

It is important that the child herself is motivated to keep her bed dry. The exercises described in this program involve a certain amount of dedication. If your child is only doing them because you want her to keep a dry bed, she's less likely to stick with it and succeed at it.

Another reason this motivation is important is because children who wet their beds often feel helpless about their problem. They've tried and they've failed to do what other children seem to accomplish effortlessly. They see themselves as incompetent. They tend to give up hope and stop believing in themselves. They are often made to feel babyish and stupid. It is important that the child regains a sense of confidence and competence. With this program, the child is put in charge of training her bladder. The more in charge she feels, the more confident she will become and the more likely she will be to succeed. You can help her with any of the details if she asks you to, but let her feel that it is her show and that she is running it. Your main role is that of cheerleader—boosting the player's confidence, letting her know that you believe in her, and being generous with applause for even the smallest improvement.

This sort of training shouldn't be started until the child is not only enthusiastic about it but able to approach it actively and responsibly. Many specialists in the area feel that these types of programs should only be commenced with children over the age of six.

The steps involved in bladder training are outlined in the following Annie Story. To add just a few extra details to them:

First, take about a fortnight to chart your child's wetting pattern. Is it every night? Is it worse some nights? Does it tie in with extra-late nights? Is there an eating or drinking pattern associated with it?

During this fortnight, your child should also be doing her bladder stretching exercise, that is, holding on for as long as possible after she feels the first urge to go to the toilet. She should do this at least once a day. This is best done at home rather than at school or a friend's house, where there would be more embarrassment about accidents. You can help by showing her how to focus on something else to distract her attention from her bladder.

She should also be doing her mid-stream interruption exercises to increase control of the bladder muscles. These should be done about ten times each time your child urinates.

About twice a week you should help your child measure her bladder capacity. This is best done by drinking lots of caffeinated drinks (for example, Coca-Cola), and eating snacks, preferably salty, to encourage her to drink more. Then your child needs to hold on and avoid emptying her bladder for as long as possible. When she finally gives in, she should empty her bladder into a container so that the output can be measured. The average child between six and twelve years old has a bladder capacity of about one fluid ounce (30 ml) per year of age. The twice-weekly bladder capacity measurements for your child are likely to vary quite a bit. Take the highest measurement as your mark and make this the measurement you are trying to improve upon.

During this time it's important to keep your child's motivation and confidence up. Rewarding her efforts is a good way to do this. Stars on a chart can be an indication of whether she's been doing her bladder-stretching and mid-stream interruption exercises regularly. Lots of praise is important, and it can be helpful to include a treat earned by the regular practice of her exercises. It is likely to take time for the results to show in a dry bed, so don't get discouraged and do keep letting your child know that she is doing a good job.

After this first couple of weeks, you might want to include a wetness alarm in the program. The function of these alarms is to alert the child to the bladder messages occurring during sleep. They do this by ringing a bell or sounding an alarm when they detect wetness. This wakes the child, hopefully in time to tighten the bladder muscles. The idea is that with practice, the child becomes more attuned to nighttime bladder messages and is able to respond to early bladder signals before the wetting has actually started.

If you are using such a device, it's important to help the child feel comfortable with it. Many children imagine it is going to deliver an electric shock or hurt them in some way. The Annie Story is constructed so that the wetness alarm section can be included or excluded, depending on its relevance.

It is also helpful to have your child go through, in her imagination, the successful sequencing of nighttime toilet visits. This will be most effective if your child is relaxed and totally absorbed in the imagery as she imagines her bladder communicating successfully with her brain and herself waking, getting out of bed, and getting to the toilet in time. To help your child become relaxed and absorbed in the imaginative experience, you might like to use the Relaxation story (Chapter 14) or a variation on it.

Finally a few dos and don'ts.

Don't get impatient. Accept that while some children may respond very rapidly, others will take some months before dry beds become commonplace. Keep up your child's morale and confidence by praising and rewarding even slight improvements in the size of the wet patch on the sheets.

Make sure that the way to the toilet is well lit at night and that your child feels comfortable going there.

Make sure your child is getting enough sleep. An overtired child is less likely to be able to wake in response to bladder signals.

Don't keep your child in diapers as a method of keeping the bed dry at night. This makes your child feel like an incompetent baby. Children often feel embarrassed and ashamed at having to wear diapers when they feel too old for them.

It's okay to have your child take responsibility for putting the wet sheets in the laundry. This should not be seen as punishment but as simply part of being a "big girl."

Don't scold your child for wetting the bed. When you are tired and harassed by the thought of yet another load of wash, it's easy to feel that she's doing this just to drive you mad. She's not. She usually hates wet beds even more than you do.

You don't need to starve your child of fluids. In fact, drinking helps your child with her bladder expansion and strengthening exercises. Allow your child to quench her thirst normally. Just before bedtime, however, it's a good idea to stay away from carbonated drinks or drinks with caffeine in them. This is because they often have an irritating effect on the bladder, making it send its "Empty me" message too soon and too often. Chocolate can also have this effect. Your child may also be particularly sensitive to other foods, such as milk, in this way. This is one of the things you should be looking out for in the initial fortnight of observation. Caffeinated drinks are used deliberately on the bladder capacity measurement mornings so that you don't have to hang around all morning waiting for your youngster to go to the toilet.

Finally, if you have two children who wet their beds in the house, let the older one use the program first and succeed before the younger one begins it. It can be a blow to the older one's already shaky confidence if she sees her younger sister succeed before she does.

## *annie story*

### Part 1

Annie was a little girl who lived in a brown brick house with her mommy and daddy and a big black dog named Blackie. The school that she went to was about twenty minutes away by bus, and all of Annie's friends had arranged to catch the same bus every day. They called themselves the 67 Club because the bus was a number 67 bus. Every day when Annie got on the bus, Lisa and Sarah were already on it waiting for her. Nancy, who was her very best friend, got on at the next stop.

Annie was particularly excited as she waited for the bus today. In her bag was a very special something that her mom had bought her yesterday. Annie had brought it to school to show her friends. The very special something was a big glossy poster of Samantha Starr. Annie and all her friends agreed that Samantha was the best, the very, very, very best girl singer in the whole wide world. Her records all went straight to the top and her videos made you want to watch them again and again.

Annie had her whole room plastered with photos of Samantha Starr. She had even stuck some photos up in Blackie's kennel, too, so that Blackie could look at them when she reclined in her kennel on her afternoon naps. And her morning naps. And her evening naps. Actually, Blackie's kennel was just a special part of Annie's room that Annie had roped off and hung sheets over. Blackie's real kennel was outside, and Blackie thought it was fit only for dogs and refused to sleep there.[1]

"Good morning, class," said Mr. Branton. He was Annie's teacher and he looked like a bulldog with a moustache. It was hay fever season and his moustache was whiffling a lot between sentences as he tried to stop sneezing.

"I (*atchoo!*) have some (*atchoo!*) good news," he said, his moustache whiffling madly. "The (*atchoo!*) date for the school (*atchoo!*) camp has been announced."

"Won't that be great!" said Nancy later as they sat in the playground. "We'll be sleeping in the same cabin. We can stay up all night and talk!"

"Yes," said Sarah. "I can't wait!"

"My mother said she can't wait either," said Lisa.

"Are you okay, Annie?" asked Nancy.

Annie looked up. "Oh, I'm fine," she said weakly. "I think camp will be—uh—great." And she managed a big smile. But all the time a voice inside her was saying, "How can I get out of camp? How can I get out of camp?"[2] And another voice inside her was answering, "You can't. You can't. You can't."

---

[1]Vary these details to suit your child. Include a superstar, comic book hero, or person your child admires in place of Samantha Starr, if you wish.

[2]Occasions that require overnight stays, such as camps and sleep-overs at friends', are often a source of great anxiety to children who wet their beds. They will usually avoid them at all costs.

Annie, you see, had a terrible secret. And that terrible secret meant that she couldn't go to camp. Because if she did go to camp, everyone would find out about her terrible secret and her friends would all hate her and laugh at her and no one would want to talk to her again.[3] Ever.

So you can understand that she was pretty worried when she went to bed that night. "What am I going to do!" she said to herself over and over until finally it sounded like "Wahmugunnadoo!"— which she didn't even realize was Australian for "What am I going to do"—and at last she fell asleep.

The first thing she noticed when she woke was that it was still nighttime. It was easy to notice this because the room was dark and only the moon and stars were visible. Annie looked over at the wall where her new poster of Samantha Starr glowed oddly in the moonlight. Samantha's blonde hair rippled as she tossed it over her shoulder. Annie stared. Then she shook her head. No, I must be seeing things, she thought. Posters can't toss their hair over their shoulders. She looked again. Samantha smiled at her. Annie's eyes started to look like two eggs sunny-side-up. Samantha Starr was beginning to step out of her poster.

"Well," said Samantha Starr, sitting down on Annie's bed. "I guess I should introduce myself. I'm Samantha Starr, but my friends call me Sam."

"H-h-h-hi," said Annie, who was still goggling. Her tongue felt like it was goggling, too. She just couldn't believe who was sitting on her bed.

"I suppose I should explain why I'm here," said Sam. She looked a bit puzzled. "The truth is, I don't know exactly why I'm here."

"Oh," said Annie. It was about all her tongue could manage.

"But I can tell you how I got here," said Samantha.

They both looked at the poster.

"Well, at least I can sort of tell you how I got here. You see, I have this godmother. She's not like your usual sort of godmother. She's . . . well, I think she's magic. You know, like a fairy godmother."

---

[3] Children commonly feel desperately ashamed of their bedwetting behavior.

Annie's tongue recovered. "She doesn't go around in a spangled white track suit, does she? I mean, instead of a fairy dress?"

Sam looked surprised. "Yes, she does. It's the new uniform for fairy godmothers. She was on the committee that designed it."

"I know," said Annie. "She's told me about it."

"So you know her, too," said Sam. She looked excited. "You're the only other person I know who knows her."

"She visited me once," said Annie. "She helped me with being scared of dogs."

"That's great," said Sam. "I've known her for years now. Ever since she helped me with school camp."

"School camp?" said Annie, suddenly remembering her terrible secret.

"Yes," said Sam. "She asked me to visit you today because she said you had a problem like I did and I could show you what to do."

"No," said Annie, shaking her head. "She must have made a mistake." It was impossible that someone like Samantha Starr would have had an awful, shameful problem like Annie's.

"Well, that's what she said—that you have a problem just like I used to have." Sam smiled at Annie. "You see, I was terrified to go to school camp because I used to wet my bed at night."

Annie gasped. She couldn't believe it. Samantha Starr used to wet her bed at night! Just like Annie![4]

"It's true," said Sam. "Not that anyone ever knew. I was always so scared my friends would find out. I used to make up excuses about why I couldn't sleep over at their houses. I was sure they'd hate me and not want to be friends with me if they found out my secret."

"Gosh," said Annie. "That is just like me."

"So," said Sam, "you can imagine I was really in a panic when I found out I had to go to school camp."

Annie nodded her head. She knew just what Sam meant.

---

[4]It is very encouraging for children to realize that people they look up to and admire once had a problem like theirs. If you had a bedwetting problem as a child, it is also helpful to share this with your child.

"And," Sam continued, "just when I was so miserable that I thought I was going to die, the godmother arrived and showed me what to do."

"Oh," said Annie, leaning forward. She was starting to get excited. "You mean there's something you can do about it?"

"There sure is," said Sam. "I'm going to show you what the god-mother showed me—how to keep your bed dry at night."

"Oh!" said Annie. She was so excited that she almost fell out of bed. "Can we start now? Please, can we start now?"

Sam gave her a hug. "Sure we can. Why don't you get me a pen-cil and paper? I want to do some drawings for you that will help you understand how to stay dry."

First Sam drew an outline of a girl. "Let's pretend that this is your body," she said. "You probably know that inside your body you have things like a heart and stomach and lungs."

Annie nodded. "We learned about those in school," she said. "They're called organs and they all have a different job to do."

"That's right," said Sam. "There are a lot of organs in the human body, all with their own job. One of the organs you might not have heard about is the bladder."

Annie shook her head. No one had told her about the bladder. "What does it do?" she asked.[5]

"The bladder's job is to collect all the urine[6] that the body doesn't need anymore. Then, when the bladder's full, it sends a message to the brain, the brain tells you to go to the toilet, and the bladder squeezes the urine out into the toilet."

"Oh," said Annie. "Well, how come my bladder squeezes the urine into my bed at night?"

"Well," said Sam, "there are a few reasons why that might be happening. At the end of the bladder is a muscle that opens

---

[5] A simple explanation of how the bladder works helps children understand their bed-wetting. It allows them to see it as a problem that has solutions which they can apply. Understanding a problem is the first step towards solving it.

[6] I have used the technically correct term, "urine." You may want to substitute "pee" or whatever word you would normally use with your child to describe urine or urinating.

and shuts the bladder. If the muscle is weak, the urine will come out before it's supposed to. So, one of the things you can do to stay dry at night it to exercise that muscle and make it strong."

"Good," said Annie. She wanted to have strong bladder muscles so that she could keep dry all night.

"Sometimes," Sam continued, "the brain doesn't get the message that the bladder needs to empty itself. If the brain doesn't get the message, it won't tell you to go to the toilet. That sometimes happens at night when your brain is asleep, so the bladder just empties itself in your bed. Later on I'm going to show you a special way to help your brain and bladder get their messages through to each other."

*Optional*[7]

"Sometimes, too, children's parents get them a special blanket that rings a bell as soon as the bladder begins to let go of its urine and that bell wakes the brain up so that you can go to the toilet."

"That sounds good," said Annie.

"Another thing you should know," said Sam, "is that the bladder is like a balloon. It's very stretchy and can hold a lot of urine. Some bladders, though, have forgotten how to stretch. They think they're full when they've only got a little bit of urine in them. If they learned how to stretch to their full size, they would be big enough to hold the urine in all night long and you wouldn't have to go to the toilet."

"Can I teach my bladder how to stretch better?" asked Annie.

"You certainly can," said Sam.

"Goody!" said Annie, and she was so excited that she jumped up and down on the bed.

"Well," said Sam. "What do you want to learn first?"

Annie thought for a minute. "I think I'd like to learn how to make my bladder muscles stronger."

---

[7]These two paragraphs are optional—they should only be included if you plan to use a bed wetting alarm with your child.

"That's easy," said Sam. "You know that the best way to make muscles stronger is to exercise them."

"Yes," said Annie. "If you lift things a lot, your arm muscles get strong and if you walk a lot, your leg muscles get strong."

"That's right," said Sam. "The best way to exercise muscles is to use them a lot. Now, the bladder muscles control the opening of the bladder. They're used to open it to let the urine out or to close it to keep the urine in. The best way to exercise them is when you go to the toilet—you use your bladder muscles to make the stream of urine stop and start and stop and start again. That exercises your bladder muscles and makes them stronger."

"That sounds easy," said Annie. "How many times should I do it?"

"Each time you go to the toilet, you should stop and start the stream of urine ten times. The only time you don't do the stops and starts is when you go to the toilet just before going to bed. Then you just let all the urine out."

"Okay," said Annie. "I'll start the very next time I go to the toilet. Soon I'm going to have the strongest bladder muscles in the universe."

"You bet!" said a little voice that seemed to come from somewhere inside her.

Annie jumped. "Who was that?" she asked, startled.

"It's me, your bladder muscle," said the little voice. "I'm glad you're going to make me strong. I'm sick of getting pushed around. I'm going to be the strongest bladder muscle you ever saw."

Annie looked at Sam. "I think my bladder muscle's talking to me," she said.

Sam didn't look surprised. "That's right," she said. "Now that you two have met, it's going to make things much easier."[8]

Sam took out a notebook, wrote "bladder muscle" in it, and

---

[8]Having a child meet her bladder in her imagination enhances the experience for her. It makes the learning experience more vivid and allows the child to have a greater sense of control.

made a check mark beside it. "The next thing we have to do," she said, "is teach your bladder how to hold more urine."

"Who, me?" said another voice. "Why do I need to hold more urine? It's much easier for me to empty my urine when I'm only half full."

"Well, it's not easier for me," said Annie sternly. "It gives me a whole lot of trouble."

"Oh," said her bladder. It sounded a bit sheepish. "I didn't realize I was getting you into trouble."

"Well, you were," said Annie. "You have to learn to get bigger so that you can keep urine in all night long without needing to empty yourself."

"How do I do that?" asked the bladder.

"How does it do that?" asked Annie. She looked at Sam.

"Well," said Sam, "when the bladder wants to empty itself, it sends a signal to the brain to let you know that it's time to go to the toilet. The next time that happens, instead of going to the toilet right away, see if you can wait for a while. Hold on for as long as you can. If you do that each time, it will teach your bladder how to hold on to its urine for longer and longer. It also teaches your bladder how to stretch so that it can hold more urine. That way it can hold its urine all through the night and not have to bother you."

"Great," said Annie. "I'm going to practice holding on every time I need to empty my bladder."[9]

"Hey, kid," said the bladder. It didn't sound too thrilled about this. "Are you sure you really want to do this? It was much easier for me when I could just let the urine out any time I felt like it."

"Well, that's too bad," said Annie, "because it was awful for me." She put on her strictest voice, like the one Mr. Branton used sometimes when the class was misbehaving. "Now I'm the boss around here and I want a dry bed at night, so I'm going to teach you how to hold your urine in."[10]

---

[9]When your child is practicing "holding on," it can be helpful to distract her attention with conversation, games, etc.

[10]This allows the child to experience herself as a competent "boss" rather than an incompetent person who wets her bed. The more competent your child feels, the more likely she is to succeed.

"Oh, all right," said the bladder a bit sulkily. "If you must, you must."

Annie felt quite excited. "I'm really looking forward to this," she said. "Is there anything else I can do?"

"Yes," said Sam. "One of the things you can do is to measure how much urine your bladder can hold. That way you can find out how big it is and you can also measure it as it stretches."[11]

"That sounds like a good idea," said Annie. "How do I do that?"

"It's easy," said Sam. "First of all, you drink as much as you can.[12] Then when you need to go to the toilet, hold on as long as you can. When you can't possibly hold on any longer, instead of emptying your bladder into the toilet, empty it into a big jar. Your mom can give you one. Then she can help you measure the urine so you can see how big your bladder is. It's best to do it in the morning. You can do that twice a week and watch as your bladder gets bigger and bigger. It might not get bigger all at once, and some bladders take longer to stretch than others, but if you keep doing it, it will learn to stretch and hold more urine.[13]

"And by the way," Sam added, "it's always a good idea to drink lots during the day because that gives your bladder more urine to practice stretching with."

"Sure thing," said Annie.

Sam took out her notebook again and wrote in it "bladder stretching and holding on" and made another check mark. Then she looked up.

"Oh," she said. "I almost forgot. There are a few things you shouldn't eat or drink in the evening before bedtime. They make your bladder ticklish and that makes it feel like letting go of its urine."

---

[11]The average child between six and twelve years old has a bladder capacity of about one fluid ounce (30 ml) per year of age.

[12]Encourage your child to drink as much as she can before measuring her bladder capacity. Carbonated and caffeinated drinks are good for this particular situation as they have a slightly irritating effect on the bladder. This will ensure that your child does in fact have the urge to urinate fairly soon after drinking. Eating salty foods will also increase your child's thirst, which is useful for this exercise.

[13]Results of bladder capacity measurements may be inconsistent. Use the largest one as your measure.

"Gosh, I don't want that to happen," said Annie.

"The things you shouldn't eat or drink before bedtime," said Sam, "are things like chocolate or cola or coffee."

"Okay," said Annie. "Will you write them down on your list for me?"

"Sure," said Sam.

She wrote them down and handed the list to Annie. "There you are," she said. "How about if you work on these exercises for the next two weeks? For some kids, just the exercises are enough to get their beds dry. Other kids need to do a few other things as well, but I can tell you about those later on. I'll come back to visit in a couple of weeks and you can tell me how you're doing."

"Great," said Annie, and she waved goodbye as Samantha shimmered back into her poster.

The next day Annie said to her mom, "I've decided I'm going to have a dry bed at night."[14]

"That's great," said her mom.

"I have a plan," said Annie and she started to teach her mom all about the bladder and the bladder muscles. She told her mom that she shouldn't eat or drink chocolate, cola, or coffee before bedtime and explained about the exercises she was going to do.[15]

"I have a good idea," said Annie's mom.

Annie looked at her mom suspiciously. Sometimes her mom's good ideas consisted of eating all the broccoli on your plate.

"Why don't we make up a big colorful chart," her mom said, "so that you can put check marks on it when you do your exercises and write down how big your bladder is getting and how long you can hold on before you empty your bladder."

"That is a good idea," said Annie. She loved doing drawings and coloring. "I'll make a very colorful chart."[16]

And so she did.[17]

---

[14]Here Annie is "taking charge" instead of being the passive victim of bed-wetting.

[15]Again Annie is in the role of competent teacher rather than person who wets her bed. The more in charge the child feels, the more likely she is to succeed.

[16]Most children love charts—they provide a source of immediate reinforcement and a concrete proof of change.

[17]At this point you might want to allow some time for your child to practice her exer-

**Part 2**

Two weeks later Annie was lying in bed waiting for Sam. She was feeling very pleased with herself and dying to tell Sam how well she had been doing her exercises. Annie tried to keep awake but she was really too sleepy. Slowly her eyes closed and she dozed off.

It was dark when she woke up. She opened her eyes and immediately looked at Sam's poster. Sure enough, that funny glow was coming from it as Samantha Starr tossed her hair back and stepped out of the poster.

"Hi," she said as she settled herself down on Annie's bed.

"I've been dying to see you," said Annie. "Look!" She showed Sam the chart she had been keeping for her exercises. "Those exercises are fun," she said. "I've been getting better and better at them."

Sam looked at the chart. "You've been doing a great job," she said.

Annie smiled. She felt proud of herself. "I'm still getting wet beds at night, but I figured that it's going to take time, like you said."

Sam nodded. "That's right. It does take time, but you're doing really well, and I know that it won't be long before you're having dry beds."

Annie nodded happily.[18]

"Now," said Sam, "remember I told you that most kids need to do some extra things as well as the exercises to keep dry at night?"

Annie nodded.

"Well," said Sam, "let me tell you about them. I know all about them because I did them, too, when I was learning to be dry at night.

"Remember what I told you about the bladder and how it stores urine?" asked Sam.

Annie nodded.

---

cises and measure her bladder capacity before proceeding to Part 2. As in the story, take two weeks to get the exercise routines established and bladder capacity measured.

[18]Of course, if your child is dry by this time, this section is unnecessary.

"Well, when your bladder gets full and needs to empty itself, it sends a message to the brain. The brain gets the message and then lets you know that it's time to go to the toilet. Sometimes at night, though, the bladder doesn't send the message loudly enough or the brain is too sleepy to hear. If the brain doesn't get the message, it won't tell you to go to the toilet, and then if the bladder decides to empty itself anyway, you'll wet the bed."

"How do you make sure the brain gets the message at night?" Annie asked.

"You have to teach the bladder and brain to talk to each other better," said Sam.

## Optional[19]

"One of the things you can do is get something called a bed-wetting alarm. You clip it onto your pajamas or your bed, and then if your bladder starts to let go of its urine, a bell or a buzzer sounds. That wakes your brain and it tells you to get up and go to the toilet. It also tells your bladder to hold the urine in until you get to the toilet."

"Does it hurt?" asked Annie.[20]

"No," said Sam, "it's just a bell or buzzer, like an alarm clock. You'll need to ask your mother to get one for you. When she does, she can show you the alarm and you can hold it in your hands and see that it doesn't hurt. It might tickle your hand, but it doesn't hurt."

"That sounds okay," said Annie. "I'll ask Mommy to get one for me."

"One of the things you can do to make the bed-wetting alarm work even better is sort of fun," said Sam.

"What is it?" asked Annie. She liked things that were fun.

"It's a game you can play. When you go to the toilet to empty your bladder, get your mother to stand nearby with

---

[19]This section is optional. Use it only if you are planning to use a bedwetting alarm with your child.

[20]Children are often fearful that the alarm will hurt them. It's important to reassure them on this point.

the alarm. When she makes the bell ring, you have to use your bladder muscles to stop the stream of urine as quickly as you can. Your mother can try to surprise you by not telling you when she's about to ring the bell, but as soon as you hear it you can stop the stream of urine straight away."

Annie smiled. "I bet my mom won't be able to trick me. I'll be too fast for her. That sounds like a good game."[21]

"One of the things you can do," Sam said, "to make the brain and the bladder talk to each other is really neat. It involves using your imagination. That's a very special part of your mind that's sort of like magic."

"Hey," said Annie, getting quite excited. "I didn't know I had any magic in me."[22]

"Oh, we all have magic in us," said Sam. "It's just a matter of believing in it and learning how to use it. If you like, I'll teach you how to use some of your magic right now."

Annie nodded eagerly.

"Okay then," said Sam, "hold on tight because we're going on a very special magic journey. We're going on an imagination journey."

"Where are we going?" asked Annie. She could hardly wait.

"We're going to meet your bladder and your brain," said Sam. "So, close your eyes, say the magic words 'abracadabra' and we're on our way."

Annie closed her eyes. "Abracadabra," she said. There was a sudden popping sound and a whoosh.

"Look," said Sam, "we're inside your body."

Annie looked. They were on a beautiful blue boat floating down a river. Annie was standing by the steering wheel. She was wearing a fancy white uniform with "Captain Annie" written on it in gold letters.

"Wow!" said Annie. "This is incredible."

---

[21]This practice is very helpful in getting the child accustomed to stopping the flow in response to the alarm.

[22]Magic is a powerful tool for children. It is exciting for them to know that they have their own special "magic."

"We're on our way to the bladder," said Sam. "Watch out for the signs."

Annie looked up. On either side of the river bank were large white signposts. One had an arrow pointing backwards. It said in big bold letters, "VISIT THE LUNGS," and then in smaller letters underneath, "A Breath of Fresh Air." Next to it another sign pointing sideways said, "CATCH THE BEST WAVES— Vacation at the Brain." The last signpost was just in front of them. It said, "YOU ARE ENTERING BLADDER COUNTY— Sit Back and Relax."

"Oh, wow!" said Annie. "This is great. What do I do?"

"Just keep steering straight ahead," said Sam. "You're doing fine."

Annie steered the boat in a straight line. "I like this," she said to Sam. "This is fun."

"You're a great captain," said Sam. Then she pointed ahead of the boat. "Just turn to the right at the arrow," she said.

Annie steered around to the right and found herself next to a little pier.

"You can tie the boat up there," said Sam. "The bladder's just ahead."

The bladder was lounging in an armchair when Annie got there.

It looked surprised to see her, but it waved lazily. "Hi, kid," it said.

"Two things," said Annie. "One, don't call me 'kid.' I'm your boss, you know, and don't you forget it."

The bladder looked startled. It jumped to its feet and stood at attention.

"Second," continued Annie, "I'm going to teach you to talk to the brain better at night."

"Sure thing, Sir, er, Miss, er, Boss," said the bladder. "How do I do that?"

"It's easy," said Annie. "You have to yell."

The bladder looked upset. "Yell?" it said. "But yelling takes energy. It's so much easier to whisper quietly."

"No," said Annie. "Yelling is what it's going to be. Whispering doesn't work. Now let me see you do it."

"Okay," said the bladder. It picked up a phone nearby, dialled B.R.A.I.N., and yelled into the mouthpiece.

Annie jumped. "That was quite good," she said. "Try it a little bit louder now."

After a few yells, Annie was satisfied. "That was good work," she said. "Now I'm going to have a talk with the brain."

The brain was looking very cross when Annie got there.

"That silly bladder," it said. "It's been yelling constantly and waking me up every time I get to sleep."

"That's because I told it to," said Annie.

"Eh?" said the brain. "Why would you do a stupid thing like that?"

"Because when it's full, it needs to wake you up so that I can get to the toilet in time."

There was silence while the brain thought about that.

"Oh," it finally said. "I guess that means you'll be wanting me to turn the volume of the telephone up."

Annie looked puzzled.

"I turned the volume down," the brain explained, "because I didn't want to be woken up."

"Well, that wasn't very brainy of you, was it?" said Annie. "Because you didn't wake up, the bladder let its urine out in my bed instead of the toilet."

"Oh," said the brain. "I guess I just wasn't thinking."

Annie started to say something, but the brain interrupted her.

"But now that I am thinking," it said hurriedly, "I'll turn the volume up as high as it will go."

"Good," said Annie. "Now I want to see you guys practice getting those messages through."

Annie stood and watched while the bladder picked up the phone and shouted, "I need to empty myself," and the brain woke up instantly, gave the order to get up, and guided Annie's feet out of bed and down the hall to the toilet.

Annie said, "Good work, guys. I'm going to come back regularly each day and watch you practice, so keep it up." And off she went, feeling very pleased.

"That was fun," she said to Samantha. "I liked that magic."

"Good," said Sam. "Now if you just keep up all the good work, soon you'll have a dry bed every night."

"Great," said Annie. "I can't wait."

"Don't forget it takes time.[23] For some kids it takes less time and for other kids it takes more time. It's hard to say how much time it will take for you, but if you keep doing all the things I told you, it will definitely happen."

"Great," said Annie. Then she had a funny idea.

"I know how to stop wetting the bed in no time at all."

"How?" said Sam, looking interested.

"Sleep on the floor!" said Annie, and they both laughed.

The next day Annie told her mom all about how she had bossed her brain and her bladder in her dream.

"That's terrific," said Annie's mom. "I'm really proud of you."

Annie beamed.

"How about if I leave the little light on in the hall so you can see your way to the toilet easily in the middle of the night?"

"Good idea," said Annie, nodding.

"I've got another idea," said Annie's mom. "Why don't we make a special calendar? Each morning we can look at your sheets and if the wet spot is smaller than usual, you can get a star.[24] If there's no wet spot at all, you can get two stars. When you have four stars altogether, you can trade them in for a special treat."

"Hey," said Annie. "That's a terrific idea. I'm going to go and make the calendar now."

A few months later it was nearly time for school camp. Annie was very excited about it. Now that she was dry at night, she was really looking forward to it.

---

[23]Remember that for some children it will take longer than for others. Don't let your child get discouraged. Reward her for effort and for every small improvement so that she has the sense that something positive is indeed happening.

[24]It is important to use a diminishing wet spot as a cause for praise. Even though the bed may still be wet, if it is less wet than usual, it is a sign that things are starting to work. Reward and recognize each such advance so that the child has a feeling of increasing confidence and competence.

"Isn't camp going to be great?" she said to Cindy, a new girl who had just joined their class.

Cindy looked miserable. "I don't think I'm going to be going to it," she muttered.

"Why?" asked Annie.

Cindy put her head down and said in a little voice that Annie could hardly hear, "Oh, um, I, um . . . I have a problem sleeping away from home."

"Why?" said Annie. "Do you get scared or homesick?"

Cindy shook her head. "No," she said. She looked very embarrassed. "It's, uh, not that. It's, ah . . ."

"Oh," said Annie, suddenly understanding. "I bet you have the same problem that I used to have."

"What do you mean?" asked Cindy, looking surprised.

"I used to wet my bed," said Annie.

"Really?" said Cindy in amazement. "Really and truly?"

"Yes," said Annie.

"You mean you wet your bed just like me?"

Annie nodded. "And I can teach you how to have a dry bed, just like a friend taught me."

"Wow!" said Cindy, almost jumping up and down with excitement. "You really can teach me how to have a dry bed?"

Annie nodded.

Cindy looked as if she was about to explode with happiness. "When can we start?" she asked.

"Anytime," said Annie and smiled.

# 6

# Compulsive and Perfectionistic Children

Lady Macbeth, whose words have been echoed by dog owners all over the world ("Out, out damned spot"), was the quintessential compulsive hand-washer. Compulsive acts are those a person feels driven to perform. Even though the actions may be rational in essence, they are repeated to the point of irrationality. Thus, using Lady Macbeth as our example, although it makes good sense to wash your hands after stabbing someone, it doesn't make sense to keep washing them over and over again. Lady Macbeth was driven not by a need to expunge any forensic evidence or even to keep her clothes clean, but by a need to purge herself of her guilty feelings.

Those of us who fall into the nonaristocratic, nonmurderous section of the population may also find ourselves prey to compulsive actions and obsessive thoughts.

In its most common form, compulsivity shows itself in little daily rituals connected with superstitions. Most of us, for instance, have avoided walking under ladders or opening an umbrella indoors, or have knocked on wood for luck. Most of us have also experienced a mild form of obsessive thinking—a tune we couldn't get out of our minds, for instance, or a conversation that kept being replayed in our heads.

Compulsivity often goes along with perfectionistic tendencies. Mild perfectionism can be an asset. When it goes too far, however, it can become a liability, draining us of time and energy without an appropriate reward. Again, most of us have experienced a dose

65

of this. It may range from spending an inordinate amount of time writing and rewriting a work proposal to spending hours in front of the mirror trying to get our hair to look just right.

For most of us, however, these compulsive or perfectionistic tendencies remain at a manageable level. They do not color our whole lives. Our days do not revolve around them. They do not drain us of time and energy. We are not unduly constrained by them.

Some people, however, become virtual prisoners of their compulsive behavior. It controls their lives and affects their relationships. Their perfectionistic standards are impossible to live up to and generally result in feelings of frustration, rage, incompetence, and failure.

It is quite normal for children to go through stages in which they show compulsive behavior. From the ages of two to seven, children play games in a rigid and ritualistic fashion. They recite chants and rhymes and can become compulsive about certain behaviors, such as not stepping on cracks on the sidewalk. These ritualistic behaviors, however, are usually integrated comfortably into the child's everyday life. It is when they become uncomfortable, or when the child becomes anxious about them, that they become a problem.

Compulsive rituals and excessive perfectionism often evolve as ways of warding off anxiety. Again, most of us have experienced this from time to time; we may keep our fingers crossed, for instance, while waiting for the winning lottery ticket to be announced. Compulsive and perfectionistic children, however, have higher and more constant levels of anxiety. Their repetitive behavior has spread out and intensified as a way of trying to contain or subdue that anxiety.

As well as reducing fear, compulsive behavior sometimes serves the purpose of postponing a feared or anxiety-producing event. Again, in normal life, this is something that most of us have experienced, for instance, obsessively straightening outfits or checking and rechecking makeup before emerging to face the party. Children may, for example, continually sharpen and arrange pencils and paper as a way of delaying the moment when they have to get started on their homework. If your child seems to be using compulsive or perfectionistic behavior to avoid having to face cer-

tain situations, it's a good idea to explore these situations and discover where the stresses lie.

Sometimes the compulsive behavior can be highly symbolic.
Ritualistically lining up objects in neat patterns may be a way of
trying to counteract a sense of turmoil or chaos within. Hand-
washing may be, as Lady Macbeth demonstrated, a way of trying
to symbolically wash away a sense of guilt. Perfectionistic children
may feel they have to be perfect in order to cover up for their perceived imperfections.

Compulsive and perfectionistic children often feel bad, dirty, or
inadequate inside. They commonly feel guilty over very minor
things. They are not comfortable with the expression of emotions.
Angry feelings are often particularly difficult for them to deal with.

Sometimes they have been brought up in an overly strict environment in which many things are labeled "bad" and "sinful."
The expression of feelings, particularly negative ones, may have
been taboo. They may have modeled themselves on obsessional
or perfectionistic parents. If parents can be helped to change such
problematic patterns of child-rearing, it can be enormously beneficial for the child.

In general, compulsive and perfectionistic children need to have
their self-esteem boosted. They need to be encouraged to express
emotions and to have their sense of guilt defused. They need to
learn to be gentle with themselves.

It is often helpful to teach them how to manage the tasks they
are afraid of and are avoiding through compulsive behavior. Teach
them how to solve problems and break down tasks into separate
components so that they can be achieved in a step-by-step fashion.
The task then becomes far less overwhelming. Set accessible goals
and standards for them so that they are not always striving for the
impossible. Teach them relaxation skills and social skills (see
Relaxation, Chapter 14, and Shyness, Chapter 7).

Be alert, too, for signs of depression, which is sometimes found
in compulsive and perfectionistic children. Professional intervention is appropriate in these instances. Professional help is also indi-
cated when despite your best efforts, your child is unable to break
the grip of distressing compulsive or perfectionistic patterns.

At the moment, two of the most commonly used therapies for this disorder are behavior therapy (some of which is featured in the following Annie Story) and drug therapy.

There are two Annie Stories included in this chapter. The first story details some psychological techniques that have proved useful for compulsive and perfectionistic children. A significant part of the story deals with the expression of feelings, particularly anger, as this is so often a problem for these children. For the relaxation component, turn to Chapter 14.

For the first Annie Story, I've used as an example the compulsive need to arrange objects in a particular order. In the story, Annie is encouraged to gradually leave things on her desk in a more and more disordered fashion. This is done through the "game" that she plays with the godmother and also through imaginary rehearsal while she is relaxed. The imaginary rehearsal used in this segment of the story involves the behavioral technique of desensitization. It is dealt with in more detail in the first book of Annie Stories in the Fear Of Dogs chapter.

Essentially, desensitization involves working out a "ladder" of fears relating to the object or situation your child is scared of. At the bottom rung of the ladder is a situation that your child can cope with comfortably, and at the top end is a situation that would have her feeling intensely anxious. With a fear of cats, for instance, the bottom rung might consist of looking at a picture of a cat in a children's book, while the top rung might be the experience of having a cat jump into her lap. In between these two rungs are a graduated series of situations relating to cats which range from mildly discomforting near the bottom to extremely anxiety provoking near the top.

The child is guided through this ladder one rung at a time, starting at the bottom. Every time she begins to get anxious, she is helped to relax and then she tries that rung again. After a few repetitions of rung-followed-by-relaxation, your child will feel more and more comfortable while contemplating or experiencing that rung of the ladder. When she feels quite comfortable and relaxed with it, she can progress to the next rung.

It's important to start with an item that she feels comfortable with and then move up slowly. This prevents her anxiety level from getting too high and becoming overwhelming. It is easier for her to learn to control anxiety by dealing with it a little at a time. As a beginner, after all, you wouldn't learn to ride a horse by getting straight on a bucking bronco.

Praise your child with each successful step she takes. The more competent she feels, the more confidently she will be able to face her fears.

Your child may also be taught to use self-talk. For example, with a hand-washing compulsion in which the child spends an excessive length of time washing her hands, she can be taught to say to herself, "Three minutes is long enough to get my hands clean." This can be done in conjunction with getting her to gradually cut more and more time off her hand-washing routine.

It is important to reward your child for her successes as they occur. A star chart is very useful. She can stick a star on for every success. For example, each time she has spent less than x minutes washing, she gets a star. When she has collected a certain number of stars, she can get a reward. Children love star charts and feel motivated and competent as they see the number of stars increasing.

The techniques described above can be used with many other compulsive behaviors.

The second story in this chapter is a fable for perfectionistic children that allows them to see their behavior in a different light. It is about a little girl who wanted to be perfect.

## annie story 1

Annie was a little girl who lived in a brown brick house with her mommy and her daddy and a big black dog.[1]

Today, Annie was running late for school. Her mom was in the other room.

"Annie! Annie!" Mom called. "Hurry up or you'll miss the bus."

---

[1]Change the details to suit your child.

"I'm coming," Annie called back. "I'm just about ready."

But she wasn't just about ready. She was dressed, she had had breakfast, and she should really have left the house fifteen minutes ago. But instead, Annie was standing in front of her desk carefully arranging all her things. There was a ruler, her three colored pencils, her two pens, a pencil sharpener, an eraser, her pink piggy bank, her book of stickers, two books, and her stapler.[2]

Annie had to arrange all these things perfectly. She didn't know quite why she had to do this. But she knew that if she didn't arrange everything in absolutely perfect order, she would feel very bad.[3] In fact, she would feel as if something awful was going to happen to her and as if she were the worst person in the whole world.

She very carefully placed the pink pig in its proper place. No, that was just a tiny bit too near the pencil sharpener. She moved the pig back again. Now the eraser was just a bit too close to the pig. She moved the eraser just the smallest bit sideways. Now she had to put . . .

"Annie!" her mother called. "You're going to miss the bus! What's keeping you?"

"I'll be right there!" shouted Annie. But she couldn't leave her desk before everything was absolutely, completely, perfectly, just right.

Half an hour later, a very miserable Annie was being driven to school by her mom.

"I don't understand, Annie," Mom said. "You're always late. It doesn't matter how early you get up, you always end up being late."[4]

Annie said nothing. She knew no one would understand about her desk and about all the things she had to do to keep from feeling bad.[5]

---

[2]I have used this as an example of compulsive behavior. If this is not appropriate to your child, substitute it with something that your child is compulsive about.

[3]Children are often unsure exactly why they have to perform compulsive acts. There is simply a sense that something bad will happen if they don't.

[4]When compulsive acts get out of hand, they take up more and more time, eating into the child's normal daily activities.

[5]Children are often quite secretive about their compulsive acts or obsessive thoughts.

Annie's teacher, Mrs. Clarke, was very cross with her.

"You're late again, Annie!" she said. "You'd better get your act together or you'll get into real trouble."

Annie sat unhappily at her desk and tried to follow the math lesson. She felt very ashamed that Mrs. Clarke had told her off in front of the whole class. She felt terrible. She was still feeling terrible that night when she went to bed. She set her alarm clock for an hour early, but somehow Annie knew that it still wouldn't give her enough time to arrange the things on her desk exactly the way they had to be.

"I wish there was some way I could feel better," she said to herself. "I wish . . . I wish . . . I wish . . ." But by the third wish, she had fallen asleep.

All of a sudden, there was a loud thud. Annie woke with a start. It sounded as if an elephant had been dropped onto her bedroom floor. She opened her eyes.

There, sitting on the floor and rubbing her back, was a very strange sight indeed. It was a lady wearing a shiny white track suit with a funny blue light floating all around her. Next to her was a long sparkly stick which was now slightly bent.

"Whoops," said the lady, still rubbing her back. "I seem to be having trouble with my landings."

Annie stared.

The lady sat up straight and patted at her blue light. Then she picked up the glittery stick and looked at it with dismay. "Poodles!" she said. "My magic wand's dented."

Annie's eyes opened wide. "Your magic wand?" she repeated.

The lady looked up. "Well, of course," she said. "What else would it be? The well-dressed fairy godmother never leaves home without it."

Annie's mouth opened wide.

"You mean you're my fairy godmother?" she asked.

The lady looked at her. "Well, if I was someone else's fairy godmother, I'd hardly be landing on your floor in the middle of the night," she said.

"Oh," said Annie. "Well, yes, I guess you're right."

The godmother picked herself up and sat down on Annie's bed. She looked at Annie.

"You have your mouth open," she said. "Was there anything you were going to say?"

Annie closed her mouth, suddenly remembering that it was rude to stare at someone with your mouth open. "Er, no, I mean . . . Well, yes."

The godmother nodded encouragingly at Annie. "Well?" she said.

"Um . . ." said Annie. There were actually thousands of things that Annie wanted to ask the godmother. What was she doing in Annie's room? Why was she wearing a track suit? Why was she having problems with her landings? Did her magic wand still work? But Annie couldn't think of them right now. All she could think of was, "Why did you say 'Poodles!'?"

"Well," said the godmother, giving Annie a funny look, "in fairy-godmother school we were taught that you must never, ever swear. So, whenever I'm cross, I simply say 'Poodles!' quite loudly and firmly and then I feel much better."

"Oh," said Annie. Then she thought for a few minutes. "You mean fairy-godmothers get angry?"

The godmother looked surprised. "Certainly, my dear. Everyone gets angry at some time or other. Don't you get angry?"

"I try not to," said Annie. "I thought it was very bad to get angry."[6]

"Heavens above," said the godmother. "Wherever did you get that idea?"

"I don't know," said Annie. "When I get angry, I think mean thoughts about people. And that's bad. That could be dangerous."[7]

"Dangerous?" said the godmother. "How do you mean dangerous?"

"Well," said Annie, "if you think mean thoughts about someone, that could hurt them."

---

[6]Compulsive and perfectionistic children often have difficulty in expressing emotions, particularly anger.

[7]Many children believe that angry thoughts are dangerous. They believe that wishing someone would get sick, for instance, can actually make them sick.

"My dear," said the godmother, and she patted Annie on the shoulder, "I think you've got things a bit mixed up there. Words can hurt people and actions can hurt people, but thoughts can't hurt people."

"Really?" said Annie. She was surprised. "You mean if I was angry at someone and I thought mean thoughts about them, they wouldn't get sick or have something awful happen to them?"

"Definitely not," said the godmother. "Mean thoughts can't make bad things happen to other people. To make bad things happen to other people, you not only have to think mean thoughts but you have to do something about them." She paused. "For instance, what was the last mean thought you had?"

"Oh," said Annie. She felt a bit worried. She wondered whether it was safe to say mean thoughts out loud. She wondered what the godmother would think of her if she knew what mean thoughts Annie sometimes had.

"Well?" said the godmother. She looked at Annie kindly. "Are you scared that I'll think you're a terrible person if you tell me your mean thoughts?"

"Yes," said Annie, grateful that the godmother had understood.

"Well, I'll tell you something," said the godmother, "I'd be more worried about you if you told me you didn't have mean thoughts. I don't know a child alive who hasn't had mean thoughts. And each of them thinks that their thoughts are the meanest thoughts in the whole world."

"Really?" said Annie. "You mean everyone has mean thoughts?"

The godmother nodded. "Certainly. It's natural to have mean thoughts when you're angry. Just as when you're happy, it's natural to have happy thoughts. And when you're sad, you have sad thoughts. People were made to have all sorts of feelings and all sorts of thoughts. It's natural."

"Oh," said Annie. "I didn't think of it like that. You mean it's all right to feel angry and all right to feel sad?"

"It certainly is," said the godmother. "Although most of us would not like to feel angry or sad all the time. That's because it's more fun to be happy."

Annie nodded. That made sense.

"Anyway," said the godmother, "tell me about your mean thought."

"Okay," said Annie. Somehow it didn't feel so bad after what the godmother had said. "Well, it happened last night. I was straightening the things on my desk when Mom called out to me that it was time to turn my light off. I said I was going to turn it right off and I meant to, but it took much longer than I thought to put all the things on my desk in exactly the right order. When Mom came in half an hour later and I was still fixing up my desk, she got very cross and told me I was being naughty and that I was just pretending to fiddle with my things so that I could stay up late." Annie stopped for breath and looked up at the godmother. "That wasn't fair of her. I wasn't being naughty and trying to stay up late. It was just that it was hard to get the things on my desk in exactly the right places. And I couldn't go to bed until they were."

"And you felt cross at your mom?" the godmother asked.

Annie nodded. "And I thought mean thoughts about her. I wished something would happen to her and make her as miserable as I was."

"Aha," said the godmother. She looked thoughtful.

For one moment, Annie was worried that she would turn and fly out of the window, saying as she went, "I don't want to spend one more minute with a girl as terrible as that. A girl who can think thoughts as mean as that!"

Instead, the godmother said, "Well, as mean thoughts go, that's only a medium mean thought."

Annie was surprised. "You mean that's not the meanest thought in the world?" she asked.

"By no means," said the godmother. "I told you, all children think their thoughts are the meanest thoughts in the world. When I was at godmother school, it was next door to the training camp for witches. Believe me, some of those thoughts would make your hair turn green. Theirs did, in fact."

"Oh," said Annie. She thought back. It was true, she had seen pictures of witches with green hair.

Annie smiled. She was starting to feel much better. "I used to think my thoughts could do terrible things," she said.

"You must have felt very bad after you had those thoughts if you thought they were so terrible," said the godmother.

Annie nodded. "I felt awful. Sometimes, if I put everything on my desk in the exact, right place, I'd feel better. That's why it always took me so long to get my desk just right. Sometimes I didn't even know why I was doing my desk like that. I just knew I'd feel awful if I didn't."

"You know, there are other children who feel like that," said the godmother.[8]

"Really?" asked Annie. She was amazed.

The godmother looked at Annie. "Sounds like your life would be a lot more fun if you didn't have to bother with your desk so much," she said.

"It sure would," said Annie. "But I don't know how to stop."

"I can show you how," said the godmother.

"You can?" said Annie. She was beginning to feel excited. It would be so good to just be able to put things on her desk and forget about them. "Gosh, if I didn't have to fiddle around with my desk so much, I could have lots more time to play. I could do all sorts of things with the time I saved and I wouldn't even be late for school! That'd be great."[9]

"It certainly would," said the godmother.

"But how will I be able to stop myself from feeling bad?" asked Annie. "If I don't do my desk just right, I feel bad. And if I feel bad, doing my desk helps me feel a bit better. For a while anyway."

"That's a very good point," said the godmother. "Why don't we sit down and make a list of the things that make you feel bad?"

"Okay," said Annie, and she opened her drawer and got out some paper and a pencil.

"Now," said the godmother, "let's write down all the things that make you feel bad."

Annie thought for a moment. Then she said, "Thinking and feeling angry things makes me feel bad."

---

[8]Children are very reassured to learn that they are not the only ones with this problem.

[9]Children need to be motivated to change.

"I know," said the godmother. "That's what we were talking about before, weren't we?" And she took the paper and wrote down "1. Feelings."

Then she said, "But remember what we said about feelings and thoughts, even angry feelings and thoughts?"

"Yes," said Annie. "They're natural and it's okay to have them."

"That's right," said the godmother and she wrote down next to number 1 in great big capital letters, "FEELINGS AND THOUGHTS ARE OKAY."[10] Then she looked at Annie and asked, "What's something else that makes you feel bad?"

Annie thought. "I feel bad when I don't do things perfectly," she said. "I hate to make any mistakes at all."

"Aha," said the godmother, and she wrote down "2. Has to be perfect. No mistakes." Then she said, "You expect to do everything perfectly every time."

Annie nodded.

"Goodness me," said the godmother, "that's a pretty tall order for a little girl. Do you know that I don't know anyone who does everything perfectly every single time? And thank heavens for that," and she gave a little snort. "They'd be the most terrible bore. No, my dear, you can't learn without making mistakes, and it's impossible to have fun if you're always trying to be perfect. You wouldn't want to go through life without learning or having fun, would you?"

"Oh," said Annie. She hadn't thought of it like that. "No, I wouldn't want to go through life without learning or having fun."

"Well, then," asked the godmother, and she wrote down next to number 2, "YOU DON'T HAVE TO BE PERFECT. MISTAKES ARE NORMAL. EASE UP ON YOURSELF."

"Anything else now?" asked the godmother.

"Those are the main things," said Annie.

"Okay," said the godmother. "Now I'm going to teach you a special way to feel better when you get worried or feel bad about things."

---

[10]This sort of list can be a help in defusing children's anxieties.

"That'd be terrific," said Annie. She felt excited to think there was a way of feeling better when she felt bad.

"It's good fun," said the godmother, and then she showed Annie how to relax and feel better.

This is an appropriate place to pause if you wish to tell this story in sections. Use the story in Chapter 14 to teach your child about relaxation before continuing with this story.

"That was great," said Annie. "I liked that."

"Well, that's something you can do any time you want to," said the godmother.

"Really?" said Annie.

The godmother nodded. "And what's more," she went on, "while you're nice and relaxed, you can go on to help yourself feel better about your desk."

"How do I do that?" asked Annie. She was very curious.

"Well," said the godmother, "you'll find that when you're relaxed, you feel much better about everything."

Annie nodded.

"So," the godmother continued, "you'll find that when you're relaxed, you'll also feel much better about your desk. It just won't bother you the way it usually does."

Annie nodded. That made sense, she thought.

"When you're relaxed," the godmother said, "there's also a special game you can play that will help you feel good about your desk."

"What's that?" asked Annie. She liked games.

"It's an imagination game," said the godmother.

"How do I play it?" asked Annie.

"Well," said the godmother, "when you're relaxed, you begin by getting a picture of your desk in your mind. Then you put one thing out of place on it. Then you imagine yourself looking at your desk with one thing out of place and feeling relaxed and not worrying about it.[11] When you're ready, you could go on to imagine two

---

[11]This is the process of desensitization. It is explained in more detail in the Fear of

things out of place and then three things and then four things and so on."

"But what if I get upset?" asked Annie.

"If you get upset, there's something you can do," said the godmother.

"What?" said Annie. It would be very useful to have something she could do if she felt upset.[12]

"Well," said the godmother, "when you get upset, it's often because of thoughts or pictures in your mind. When your mind makes scary pictures or thoughts, you feel nervous. So, all you have to do is change the pictures or thoughts in your mind to nice ones and you'll feel better."

"That sounds easy," said Annie.

"Now, what could be a happy picture that you could think of?" asked the godmother.

"I could think about Disneyland," said Annie. "Or I could think about going ice-skating next Saturday."

"Good," said the godmother. "They sound like fun things to think about. So, if you get upset, you just stop thinking about your desk and think about your happy things until you're feeling good again. Then, when you're relaxed, you can go back to thinking about your desk again. Each time you do it, it gets easier and easier."

"That sounds neat," said Annie. "I'd like to try some of that."

"Okay," said the godmother. "We can do that now if you like."

So Annie and the godmother played the imagination game.

Annie imagined herself putting things out of place on her desk.[13] Whenever she felt nervous, she just switched to imagining herself ice-skating. She skated all around the rink without even holding on.[14] Then she would go back to imagining her desk again.

---

Dogs story in the first volume of Annie Stories.

[12]Children feel much more confident when they have a technique they can use to control anxiety.

[13]Take care to move at the child's pace. Don't hurry things along—only move on to the next item when your child is able to imagine the previous one and feel relaxed about it.

[14]This just happens to be my daughter's current goal. Modify this to suit your child.

"You're right," she said to the godmother, "this makes it a lot easier. I like this imagination game."

"You're very good at it," said the godmother. "You have an A + excellent imagination. You can do lots of terrific things with it."[15]

Annie was having a lot of fun playing the imagination game, and she was surprised when the godmother suddenly looked at her watch.

"Whoops, I must fly," she said. "It's almost midnight."

Annie looked disappointed.

"I'll tell you what," the godmother said. "I'll come back tomorrow to teach you some more ways to feel okay about your desk."

"Great!" said Annie happily.

"Bye, bye," said the godmother. And she was off through the window.[16]

Annie couldn't wait for the godmother's visit the next night. She had practiced her relaxation during the day and was feeling great. She was really looking forward to telling the godmother about it. She was also looking forward to feeling better about her desk.

She had just closed her eyes, when a large thump woke her. It wasn't quite as loud as yesterday's thump but it was still a thump.

Annie opened her eyes and there was the godmother, sitting on the floor and looking quite pleased with herself.

"I think my landings are getting better," she said. She rubbed her back thoughtfully. "Hmm . . . Yes, a definite improvement over yesterday."[17]

"I've been doing my relaxation and imagination," said Annie. "It's fun."

"Good," said the godmother. "Are you ready to have some more fun?"

"You bet," said Annie. "Are you going to teach me more ways to feel better about my desk?"

"I certainly am," said the godmother. "What we're going to do

---

[15]Praise and reinforcement are very important. As well as helping motivate your child, they also build up her self-esteem.

[16]This is an appropriate place to pause if you wish to tell the story in sections.

[17]The Godmother is a role model for not getting upset over imperfections.

is play another game. It's lots of fun and it will also help you with your desk."[18]

"Good," said Annie.

"First," said the godmother, "go over to your desk and see whether everything is in perfect order."

"It is," said Annie.

"Now," said the godmother, "I'm going to close my eyes, and while I do that, I want you to put one of the things on your desk in the wrong place, and then I have to see if I can pick which one it is."

"Okay," said Annie. Then she stopped. "What if I feel bad after I've moved one of the things on the desk into the wrong place?"

"If you feel bad, you could do your relaxation," said the godmother. "Or you could think about fun things, or you could start your jigsaw puzzle, or draw a picture. They would keep your mind busy so it won't have time to think about your desk.[19] You could tell yourself that your desk is okay the way it is,[20] and you could also find another, nicer thought to pop into your mind instead."[21]

"Okay," said Annie. She liked knowing that there were things that she could do to feel better.

"All right," said the godmother. "I'll close my eyes now."

Annie went over to her desk. She decided to move her pencil sharpener so that it was a little bit crooked. She felt a bit funny when she moved the sharpener, but it felt okay.

"I'm ready," she said to the godmother.

"Okay," said the godmother, "here I come. I bet I can spot it in six seconds!"

Annie giggled. This was going to be fun. "I bet you can't," she said.

The godmother took longer than six seconds. Annie decided to pass the time by doing her relaxation. She used her imagination to take herself off to Disneyland and was having so much fun that

---

[18]Making this a game helps to defuse the tension and also makes it more fun.

[19]Distractions can help keep your child's mind off the desk. Teaching your child how to distract herself is helpful.

[20]This is self-talk. For more details, see Chapter 11 on Impulsive Children.

[21]Substituting a positive thought for an anxiety-arousing thought is helpful.

she got quite a surprise when the godmother said, "Got it! It's the pencil sharpener."

"That's right," said Annie.

"Okay," said the godmother. "Now it's your turn again. This time you can move two things while I close my eyes."

"I bet it'll take you longer than six seconds to guess," said Annie.

"I bet you're right," said the godmother. "You're good at this game."

"It's a fun game," said Annie.

By the time Annie got to move four things on her desk, she thought it was the best game she'd played for ages. Annie wanted to keep playing but the godmother had to go.

"I must fly," she said. "But I'll be back tomorrow. What you can do, though, is to leave one thing out of place in the morning. I'll see if I can spot it when I visit you tomorrow night."

"Okay," said Annie. "I'll leave one thing out of place before I go to school."

When the godmother came the next night, it took her a couple of minutes to spot what was out of place. "You really are very good at this," she said. "How about tomorrow morning, you leave two things in the wrong place?"[22]

"Okay," said Annie. She felt pleased with herself.

By the end of the week Annie was leaving six things out of place and it was taking the godmother longer and longer to work out which place they should be in. Annie was very pleased with herself. She was having fun putting things in the wrong place.

On the last night of the week, the godmother said, "I give up. You're so good at mixing these pieces up, that I can't figure out where they should be."

Annie was delighted. She laughed at the face the godmother made as she tried to remember what should be where.

---

[22]If you are doing this with your child, you might like to construct a star-chart, where she gets a star for every object she leaves out of place. If she collects a certain number of stars, she gets a reward. This technique can be used for other compulsive behavior, for example, a star for every 30 seconds she is able to clip off excessive hand washing time.

"This is great," Annie said. And then she thought of something. "You know, it's funny. I've been having so much fun playing this game that my desk hasn't worried me at all. When I was doing this morning's game, I just mixed all the things up and left for school. I wasn't worried that things weren't in the right place."

"That's terrific!" said the godmother. "I'm really proud of you."

"Me, too," said Annie. And she smiled a great big smile.

## *annie story* 2

Annie was a little girl who lived in a brown brick house with her mommy and her daddy and a big black dog.[1]

Annie's house was built in a large, square shape, with paths running up either side of it. The first path led to the front door, which was brown with a little round buzzer on it that looked like an M & M but didn't taste as good.

The other path led to the witch's room.

The witch's room was a tiny little window facing out of the left side of the house and into the bushes and trees. Part of Annie knew that it was only the bathroom window, but the other part knew that it was where the witch lived.

Annie had never seen the witch, but she knew that she was there. She knew this because of the way her tummy felt every time she went too far down that path and got too close to the narrow little window and too close to the grasping bushes and trees.

Annie knew that the easiest way to avoid witches was to do things very, very carefully. She knew that witches hate neatness and even numbers and niceness and not stepping on cracks. So Annie knew that if she could do all these things and do them all the time, the witch couldn't get her. All day long she practiced being neat and nice. She was always polite and always said thank you. Even when she was mad at someone, she always said thank you, because she knew that witches liked madness and messes and

---

[1]Change the details to suit your child.

murder and misery, and who knew what not saying thank you might lead to?

When she walked, Annie counted her steps to make sure they ended in an even number. If it looked like there weren't enough steps, she would add a tiny little one, a baby step, to make up the numbers. She never stepped on cracks, either, because she had heard the children say that stepping on cracks would break your mother's back and the witch would like that.

It took up a lot of time, counting and not stepping on cracks, but it made Annie feel safe, or at least safer. And all the time she kept thinking about ways to feel even more safe. She knew that witches hated people being perfect, because if you were perfect they couldn't get you. So Annie tried to be perfect in every way. It took a lot of energy because if there was even the tiniest little thing that she wasn't perfect in, the witch could sneak up and get her. So everything had to be just so.

You can see that she was kept very, very busy—counting steps, not stepping on cracks, and being absolutely perfect—and you would think that with all these things to do, she would feel very, very safe. But sometimes, when Annie was coming into the house up one path, she would look to her left at the other path, to where it hobbled along like knobbly, old knees underneath the rose bushes, and get a little, scary shiver running all down her back as if her hair had suddenly melted into ice-cold rain.

One day Annie woke up feeling very peculiar. Her head felt as if someone had sneaked inside it during the night and was knocking around bashing on the walls of her forehead and generally making the sort of fuss you would rather not have being made in your head. Annie's forehead felt very hot, too, and her face looked flushed as though she had just been running.

"Goodness," said Annie's mom, when she saw her. "You don't look well at all. I think you'd better stay home in bed today, young lady."

"Bother," said Annie. "Bed's boring." And she sat up to get out of bed. But when she did that, the room went round and round like a washing machine and she had to lie down again.

"At least I'm not a T-shirt," she thought to herself. "Life must be rotten for them." And she thought about her T-shirt going round and round in the washing machine until she made herself even more dizzy and finally fell asleep again.

When she woke, her mother was standing by her with a huge glass of orange juice.

"Here, darling," she said. "It's good to drink when you're sick."

"I might do some drawing," Annie said to her mom. "Will you bring me my pencils and paper, please?"

Her mother went off to get them. That was one of the good things about being sick. You got to order your mom around.

Annie sharpened her pencil—it was black with a triangular eraser on top—and thought about what to draw.

She decided to draw some children playing. There were two girls, about Annie's age. They wore very pretty dresses with lots of ribbons and bows.

Annie drew very, very carefully, because of course everything had to be perfect. Every time she made even the tiniest mistake, she erased it very hard and started all over again. Soon the children were perfect, even to the last eyelash. Then she drew a perfect house for them to sleep in and a perfect lawn for them to play on and a perfect lake for them to swim in. While she was drawing the path leading from the lawn to the lake, she had some trouble. She had been trying to make the path look like bricks and instead it just looked bumpy and knobbly. When she tried to erase it, it got smudged and looked even worse. She got very cross with herself. She erased some more and then some more. The more she tried, the grubbier the path looked. Annie could feel the tears coming to her eyes. Her beautiful, perfect drawing was all ruined. She put her pencil down on the page and sobbed and sobbed, and then suddenly fell asleep.

When she woke, she was in a strange land. Everything looked different, although, oddly enough, it also looked very familiar. Stretching out on all sides of her was a carpet of green grass. And it really did look like a carpet. Every blade was the same bright green and they all stood up perfectly straight at exactly the same height, as if someone had gone around with nail scissors and clipped every one of them just so. About six feet to Annie's left was a bright blue lake. It was so shiny and still that it looked as if someone had poured blue jelly into it instead of water. It sat under the sun and shone. Annie wondered if it would melt.

Just beyond the lake were some trees. They were the most beautiful trees Annie had ever seen. Each one was a perfect shape, the kind you see on postcards but never in real life. The bark of the trees looked like rough velvet, the leaves were a beautiful, polished green, and each tree held its arms up and posed as if it were about to be photographed for an expensive fashion magazine. Annie caught her breath. She had never seen anything like this before. It was wonderful. It was perfect.

She moved closer for another look, and just as she did so—"Aaargh!" came an explosion from near her feet. Then there was a pitiful, weak scream. Annie stared at the ground. What was happening? Who was in trouble? She couldn't see anyone.

"Help, help!" the pitiful voice screamed.

"Little creep!" snarled a nasty, knifelike little voice. It was the sort of voice you could imagine being slipped into your back as you crept down a dark alley in the dead of night. "Think you'll come and disturb us, do you! Well, you'd better think again!" And there was a terrible, ripping sound. The screaming stopped.

Annie dropped to her knees to see what was going on.

"Ha, ha, ha!" shrieked a multitude of reedy little voices. "We got him, we got him! Little sneak! Thought he'd get through us, did he?"

Annie jumped, which was a little difficult because she was still on her knees. It was the grass speaking! A number of the fine green blades were now waving viciously and holding up a small purple weed. Its roots dangled helplessly from the grip of the grim, green spear-tips. Annie snatched it up and stood up. The grass rippled with shock.

"Where is it? What's happened?" it shrieked.

Annie stood defiantly, waiting to be discovered. But nothing happened.

"Maybe it can't see me," thought Annie. "Maybe I'm too big for it to see. It can probably only see little things, things that are its own small size, and it misses out on all the bigger things in its world."

The weed wriggled feebly in Annie's hand. "Thank you," it said in a weak little voice. "If you plant me, I'll grow for you. I make very pretty purple flowers."

"I'm sure you do," said Annie. "But there doesn't seem to be anywhere that I can plant you right now. I'll put you in my pocket for now. It's dark and safe there and you can sleep until I find the right spot."

"Thank you," said the weed, snuggling its roots into a nice round little ball so that it could fit cozily into Annie's pocket.

"I wonder if those trees would provide some shelter for my little weed?" Annie thought, and headed toward them.

The sky was as blue as china and the sun was beginning to get hot. A bird flapped lazily toward them like a swimmer in the sky.

"Perhaps it has a nest in the tree," thought Annie as the bird prepared to land on one of the branches.

Suddenly there was a loud "thwack," a squawk, and an enraged high-pitched screaming.

"Get off my leaves, you feathered fathead," the tree shrieked. "You flying flopwit, you've ruined my hairdo, you fatuous flitterbrain."

The bird was flying through the air backwards with a startled look on its face. This was because it had been bopped abruptly by the tree branch which had bent backwards and flicked the bird like an arrow from a bow or a stone from a slingshot.

The tree was shaking its leaves and saying crossly to itself, "Well, I never! Just back from the hairdresser—" when there was a sudden splash. The bird had landed in the lake.

"Aaargh," came a choking, gurgling screech. The water in the lake stood up in startled, jumping waves. "You're making me ripple! You're making me ripple!" the voice screamed. "Get out!" And the bird suddenly rose up from the waves as if a giant hand had picked it up and batted it into the sky. It hovered uncertainly in the air for a second, then, with a last horrified glance, it turned rapidly and sped for the horizon.

Annie released her breath. "Oh, my goodness," she thought. "What a strange and dangerous world."

"Whatever will I do now?" she wondered and looked around her. Over to her left there was a house. It was a very modern looking house, with brick walls and a pleasant, bushy garden. "Perhaps the person who lives there can help me," thought Annie and she set off toward it. To get there she had to pass by the lake again. It was smooth and shining once more. Annie walked cautiously by its edge. She hated to think of what would happen if she fell in.

There was a quacking sound behind her. Annie turned. A group of ducks were walking by, a mother and five ducklings. One of the ducklings was saying in a whiny voice, "I hate water. It pushed me out, you know."

The mother duck turned toward Annie. "Children," she said with a long-suffering look. "What can you do with them? Always some sort of trouble. The last one turned into a swan! What's a mother supposed to do?" And she walked wearily on. She was almost around the bend when she stopped and turned back. "Aren't you cold, little girl?" she called out in her strange honking voice.

Annie nodded, for indeed she had just realized that she was. For some reason, she seemed to be dressed in her pajamas, and not very clean ones at that. They had orange juice stains on them and black pencil smudge marks.

"There's a cloak just up ahead on that road," called back the duck. "A little girl left it there this morning. I'm sure she won't mind if you borrow it." And then the duck turned off around the bend, the five little yellow ducklings following her.

The cloak was exquisite. "The little girl who owns this must be very happy," thought Annie. "Imagine getting to wear clothes like this every day. She must take very good care of them, too." For it was true, there wasn't even the tiniest speck of dust or dirt, not even the smallest suggestion of crayon, not even the faintest hint of a crease to spoil the cloak's perfection. Annie put it on. She felt like a princess. Although it was hard not to keep worrying that somehow she would get it dirty. Especially when she thought of the state of her own clothes underneath.

A little snore came from her pajama pocket underneath the cloak. It was the weed. It had obviously gone to sleep. "Well, at least it was lucky I had these pajamas on," thought Annie. "I could never have kept the weed anywhere on this beautiful cloak. Perhaps I could plant it in that garden over there." For she was quite close to the house by now and was just about to turn in at the gate when a shout stopped her.

Annie turned around. There were two little girls running toward her. They were both dressed in the most beautiful clothes. Their hair was combed in perfect curls and waves, their shoes were spotless, and their socks stretched effortlessly up to just the right place on their ankles.

Annie caught her breath. They looked as if they had just stepped out of a storybook illustration. She pulled her cloak tighter around her so that her pajamas wouldn't show. Whatever would they think of her if they could really see what she looked like? She stood hanging her head and feeling very shy as the girls came up to her.

"I'm Julie and this is Susan," said the taller girl.

"I'm Annie," said Annie. The two girls looked even more perfect close up. How lucky they were, thought Annie. It was obvious that they didn't need to try to be perfect. They just seemed to be made that way.

"Listen," said Julie, "it's best not to go into that house."

Susan nodded her head in agreement.

"But why?" asked Annie. She looked closer at Julie and Susan. It was strange, but they didn't seem very happy at all. If Annie was as perfect as Julie and Susan, she would be very happy all the time, she was sure. Why weren't they? She looked at the house again. It looked absolutely fine. "Why shouldn't I go in there?" she asked again.

"It's hard to say," said Julie.

"It sounds silly," said Susan, "but it's just best not to go in there." She looked frightened.

"I don't understand," said Annie. "Whose house is it?"

"It's our house," said Julie.

"But it's changed," said Susan. "Now when we go inside, the

carpet rolls back like a tongue and spits us out. It says it doesn't want footprints on it."

"The bed throws us off and yells at us for messing it up," said Julie.

"And the kitchen won't let us get any food from it because it says it's just been cleaned," added Susan. She looked close to tears.

"But . . . " said Annie. She had been about to say, "But that's silly," when she remembered the grass and the weed, the tree and the bird, the lake and the ducks. "But when did this happen?" she asked instead.

"This morning," said Julie and Susan. "When the witch came."

Annie stared. A cold fragment of fear rustled its way up and down her neck and whispered, "The witch is here. The witch is here."

"Everything was normal before then," said Julie. "We wore normal clothes and did normal things."

"Some things we were very good at and some things we weren't so good at. But we tried," said Susan, "and," she pointed at her dress and burst into tears, "we didn't have to be like this!"

Julie nodded. "When the witch came," she said, "everything changed. Everything had to be perfect. If it wasn't, it just got . . . vanished!"

"Vanished?" said Annie. It sounded terrible.

"Yes," said Julie. "The witch's broomstick would come down from the sky and 'poof!' there would be nothing there."

"We were so scared," said Susan. "We were scared to get our clothes dirty or creased in case we vanished, too."

"The grass wouldn't let us sit on it, the lake wouldn't let us swim in it, the house wouldn't let us live in it. The only thing that would let us be on it was this little path."

Annie looked down at her feet. Sure enough, they were all standing on a rough, knobbly, rather smudged-looking path. It looked very familiar.

"How do you know it was a witch?" asked Annie. She was beginning to remember something.

"Because of her broomstick," said Julie. "See, she's parked it in the sky." And she pointed up toward a long thin shape with a point on one end and a triangle on the other. It was black and lay perfectly still, covering the righthand corner of the bright blue sky.

"Oh!" said Annie, because she had suddenly remembered. "That's not a witch's broomstick! That's my pencil with an eraser on the end!"

The children looked at her in disbelief.

"It's true!" said Annie. "I drew you this morning. And I wanted so much for everything to be perfect, I rubbed out anything that wasn't. I thought it would feel good to be perfect. I thought if you were perfectly perfect, you would feel perfectly good." She shook her head. "But it doesn't work that way, does it. You just spend all your time worrying about keeping perfect, and you forget to enjoy all the things that aren't perfect."

The children still looked disbelieving.

"It's all true!" said Annie. "It really is my pencil. I know! I'll prove it to you. Look, I'm going to take off my cloak and underneath it I'm wearing my pajamas that are grubby from the orange juice I spilled this morning and the pencil I smudged when I drew you."

"Don't!" said Julie. She looked terrified. "The witch will rub you out!"

"I'm scared!" said Susan. She hid her face in her hands. "I don't want anyone else to get vanished."

"It's all right," said Annie. "It's really all right. No one will get rubbed out anymore. Look!" And to Julie and Susan's horror, she slipped off her cloak.

Nothing happened. No witch came down out of the sky. No terrible magic was performed. There was just Annie, smiling in her old pajamas and Julie and Susan looking increasingly delighted as they realized that Annie was right.

"Oh!" squeaked Susan. "I'm so happy."

"Me too!" said Julie. She grabbed Annie's hand and danced round with her. "Annie, you're wonderful!"

And they danced round and round.

"Goodness," said Annie's mom as she came into the room carrying a bowl of hot soup. "You've had such a long sleep. And you're looking a lot better, too."

Annie nodded. "I feel much better," she said.

"It's such a nice, sunny day today that I think you could go out and play in the garden after your soup," said Annie's mom. She opened the curtains. The sunlight flooded in.

Annie wandered into the garden. The sunshine leaked through the leaves like drips of hot butter. Even the witch's path looked different. Everything looked peaceful. Suddenly there was a faint, little snore from Annie's pocket.

"The weed!" thought Annie. "It's still in my pocket!" And she felt inside. Sure enough, a sleepy voice said, "Is it morning already?"

"Hello, weed," said Annie. "We're back home at my place. And I've got just the right place for you to live." And she moved over to the witch's path. Now that she was close, she could see that it was indeed the same friendly, knobbly path that had been kind to Julie and Susan. Next to it was a rich, inviting patch of earth.

"I'm going to plant you here," said Annie. "And then whenever I look at this path, the first thing I'll see will be your beautiful purple flowers. And I'll remember."

And she did.

# 7
## Shyness

Shyness is far more common than most people, particularly shy people, imagine. Some studies show that approximately 40 percent of teenagers and adults describe themselves as shy. The next time you or your child is struck by an attack of shyness, look around the room; it may be comforting to know that even if they're not showing it, a sizable proportion of the people you see are feeling the same way you do.

Someone once described shyness as the mildest form of paranoia. Shy people imagine that everyone is looking critically at them or would be if they noticed them. The shy person's solution is usually to try to stay as inconspicuous as possible.

Shy people are acutely self-conscious and their sense of self is often quite negative. Thus, they feel glaringly aware of their faults, both real and imagined, and unaware or unappreciative of their strengths. They are often thin-skinned, that is, particularly sensitive to criticism and implied criticism.

When working with shy children, it is important not only to teach them the appropriate social skills but also to build up their self esteem. Shy children often put themselves down, so they need help in recognizing their assets. It can be helpful to make a list of their strengths and abilities. Praise is tremendously important. Showing your child that you think highly of her helps her to think highly of herself.

In social situations, shy children often shrink from interaction with others. They feel anxious and inferior to the other children. They are often hesitant to try new things; they don't take the initiative or assert or defend themselves. They often present themselves badly, with poor communication skills and excessively submissive body language.

The shy child thus often falls into a vicious trap of self-fulfilling prophecy. Her mannerisms and approach all indicate her expectation of rejection by others, and this in fact makes them more likely to reject her. The more she holds back or is rejected, the more likely she is to remain shy, due to both lack of practice and lack of positive feedback. So the teaching of social skills and the encouragement of practice of these in everyday situations is very important.

When teaching social skills to shy children, it is helpful to be able to demonstrate nonshy behavior to them. Children learn better when they can actually see what they should be doing and when they have someone to model themselves on. If you yourself are shy—many shy children have shy parents—look around you to see if there are appropriate family members or friends whom you can enlist as teaching aids. If there's no one appropriate, you and your child may be able to learn together by watching how socially confident people behave and what they say. Take notice of their body language as well as their words. You might also be able to find a social skills or assertiveness class that you can attend and share your learning with your child.

It is important to distinguish the shy child from the child who is simply less outgoing and prefers solitary activities. These self-sufficient children may be perfectly happy with their lives, in contrast to shy children who experience themselves as being on the outside yearningly looking in. They would like to enjoy friendships and social activities but are prevented from doing so by their fear and lack of confidence.

It is also worth noting that it is normal for young children to go through periods of shyness at certain stages. Around five to eight months and again at two years, for instance, many children become shy. This shyness doesn't last, however, in contrast to the shy child, whose shyness is a stable characteristic.

Because shy children are rarely disruptive and usually cause misery only to themselves, they often go unnoticed. Given the frustrations, sadness, and unfulfilled potentials that can go hand in hand with shyness, it's worth watching for. Some extra time and energy may help your youngster gain the confidence needed to take part comfortably in the various social situations of everyday life.

*annie story*

Annie was a little girl who lived in a brown brick house with her mommy and her daddy and a big black dog.[1]

Annie went to school near her home. She caught a big bus to school every morning. Annie liked school, but she also didn't like it. The part she liked was learning things and making things and doing projects. The part she didn't like had to do with the other kids. It wasn't that Annie didn't like the kids. She did like them. It was just that she didn't like herself when she was with them. When she was with the other kids, she felt really stupid. She didn't know what to say or do or how to act. Everything she thought of sounded dumb. All of the other kids seemed to know exactly what to say to each other. They joined in whatever game was going on. They laughed and told jokes with each other. Annie wished she knew how to do that. She wished she were brave enough to join in and play games with them or even speak to them in the easy way they spoke to each other. But she knew she couldn't. She didn't know how.

Every time she was with a group of kids, she was sure they all hated her and thought she was dumb.[2] She thought they would never want to play with her or talk to her. She felt like a nobody; actually, she felt worse than a nobody. Nobody's were invisible because they weren't there. Annie felt very visible. She thought people were staring at her and thinking to themselves how ugly she was, and how boring and clumsy, and how they wished she wasn't there.

When Annie came into a room, she always tried to make herself less visible. She would hunch her shoulders down to make herself look as small as possible. She would never look anyone in the eyes. And if she had to speak, she would speak in the softest, tiniest voice as if she really weren't there at all.[3]

---

[1] Change the details to suit your child.

[2] Shy children often imagine that anything they do will attract immediate and derogatory attention. They feel very conspicuous. They will often perceive rejection even when it isn't there.

[3] This sort of body language doesn't invite friendly contact.

One day Annie came home from school and said to her mother, "What does 'shy' mean?"

"Why do you ask?" her mom said.

"My teacher said I was shy," said Annie.

"What do you think it means?" asked her mom.[4]

Annie thought for a moment. "Well," she said, "I think it means being quiet and never saying things in class."

Her mom nodded.

Annie went on, "I think it also means being scared to join in and talk with the other kids. I think it means someone who wants to join in but who doesn't know how and thinks it's scary."

Her mom looked at Annie. "Is that how you feel, honey?" she asked.

Annie nodded.

Her mom gave her a hug. "That doesn't sound like a whole lot of fun for you," she said.

"It's not very nice," said Annie. "I feel really miserable when I watch the other kids play and I'm too scared to join in."

"What scares you about joining in?" asked her mom.

"I'm scared they'll think I'm stupid," said Annie. "I'm scared they won't want to play with me. I'm scared that I'll look like an idiot because I won't know what to say or do."

"That sounds like a lot of scary things," said her mom.

Annie nodded miserably.

"You know," said her mom, "lots of kids feel just like you do."[5]

"Really?" said Annie. She was very surprised to hear that.

"It's true," said her mom. "Lots and lots of kids."

"Gosh," said Annie. "I thought I was the only one." It felt a bit better to know that there were other kids who felt like her.[6]

"And," said her mom, "did you know that there are lots of

---

[4]It's useful to find out what your child would classify as 'shy' behavior.

[5]Most shy children feel as if they are the only ones they know burdened with this problem. It's useful to point out to them how many shy people there really are. It's also worth pointing out that there are many people who were shy and have overcome it. If you fall into this category, it would be very helpful if you could share your experiences with your child.

[6]Children can be very reassured to find that they are not the only one who feels like this.

things you can do to help yourself feel better so that you can join in with the other kids and speak up in class?"

"Really?" said Annie. Her eyes opened wide. "Are there really things I can do to feel better?"[7]

"There sure are," said her mom. "Would you like me to tell you about them?"

"Wow," said Annie. "You bet."

"Well," said her mom, "why don't we start at the beginning? Tell me what happens when you're at school and the kids are playing and you want to join in but you're scared."[8]

"Well, nothing really happens," said Annie. "I just sort of stand there and watch them. I don't do anything. Nothing happens."

"Show me how you stand there," said her mom. "Just pretend that you're at school doing it right now."

"Okay," said Annie. And she stood there with her shoulders slumped and her head down, pretending she was at school watching the other kids playing.

"See," she said to her mom. "I don't do anything. Nothing happens."

Her mom shook her head. "No, Annie," she said, "there's actually quite a lot happening."

Annie looked puzzled. "I don't understand," she said.

"Well, honey," her mom said, "you think that because you didn't say anything, nothing happened. But did you know that humans can actually say quite a lot without using their voices?"[9]

"That sounds weird," said Annie.

"Well, you watch," said her mom, "and see if you can understand what I'm saying."

"Okay," said Annie. She was curious to see what would happen.

---

[7]Children often feel powerless to change; it is helpful for them to know that there is something they can do.

[8]Pick a "shy" behavioral pattern that your child would like to change. Ask her to describe and act out that behavior so that you and she can see exactly what she is doing.

[9]It can be quite a revelation to children to discover the messages they have been sending through body language. It can be exciting for them to learn that they can change these messages.

"Now, I'm not going to say a word," said her mom, "but I think I'll still get my message through."

Then Annie's mom put on a really mean face. She narrowed her eyes and stared at Annie. She made her lips go thin and tight. She put her hands on her hips and glared at Annie.

"Golly!" said Annie. "You're saying that you're angry!"

"That's right," said her mom, "and I didn't have to say a word out loud."

"Hey," said Annie. "That's neat. Can you do some more?"

"Okay," said her mom. "What am I saying now?" And she opened her eyes wide. Her eyebrows arched up and her mouth opened in a big O shape.

"You're surprised!" said Annie. "You're saying you've had a surprise."

"That's right," said her mom. "And what about this one?" And she looked up at Annie with a bright smile. Her eyes sparkled and creased at the edges with smile lines. She looked Annie straight in the eye and looked really pleased to see her.

"I know what that is," said Annie. "You're saying that you're happy and you're pleased to see me."

"You got it," said her mom. "What about this one?" And she hunched her shoulders over and hung her head down. She wouldn't look Annie in the eye. Instead she just looked down at her feet. She had a miserable expression on her face.

"I know that one," said Annie. "You're saying that you're feeling unhappy and you don't feel like talking to anyone."

"That's right," said her mom. "Now, I have a question to ask you. If two kids came up to you and one of them looked like this," and her mom smiled and looked Annie in the eyes, "and the other one looked like this," and she hunched her shoulders and looked down at her feet, "which one would you rather play with?"

"The first one, of course," said Annie. "The one who smiled and seemed to like me."

"Yes," said Annie's mom, "I think most people would agree with you." She paused. "Now," she said, "I'm going to ask you a very important question and I bet you can answer it." She made the sad face with her shoulders hunched over and her eyes fixed on her shoes. "The question is," she said, "where have you seen that look before?"

Annie thought. Then all of a sudden she said, "Oh!"

Her mom looked at her.

"That's the way I look when I'm hanging around other kids!" said Annie. She looked at her mom. "Do you mean that I'm giving them a message even when I haven't said a word?"

"It seems like that," said her mom. "And it sounds as if you're giving them a message that you don't really want to give."

"Yes," said Annie. "I'm giving them an 'I'm miserable and I don't feel like playing' message, when what I'd really like to give is a 'I really like you guys and I'd love to play' message."

"That's right," said her mom. "Now think back to the kids at school and the way they ask the others to play. Which one gives the message that you'd like to give?"

Annie thought. "Janet," she said.

"Well," said her mom, "how does Janet look when she asks the others to play? Why don't you pretend you're Janet and that you're asking me to play?"[10]

"Okay," said Annie. This was sort of fun. She held her head up and put her shoulders back instead of slumped over. She looked her mom in the eye and smiled. "Would you like to play?" she said.

Her mom nodded. "That was great, Annie," she said. "And did you notice that when you spoke, your voice was louder than it usually is?"

"Yes," said Annie. She had noticed. She had spoken louder because that was how Janet spoke. She didn't whisper like Annie usually did.

"You know," said her mom, "when you asked me to play, your voice sounded happy and confident."

Annie nodded. "It was easier than I thought," she said. "I just pretended that I was an actress, and I was acting being Janet."

"Well, you're a very good actress," said her mom.[11] "That was

---

[10]It is useful for the child to have a successful role model to imitate and learn from.

[11]Surprisingly enough, a lot of shy children like acting. Being on stage allows them to become absorbed in a different role and to lose their excessive self-consciousness.

terrific. Acting is a good way to practice looking confident and happy. And you know what? If you practice it long enough, after a while you'll find that you really are feeling confident and happy when you talk to people."

"Really?" said Annie. This sounded good.

"I have an idea," said her mom. "Why don't we see if we can pick out some of the important things you did that made you look happy and confident instead of shy and miserable? Let's see how many things we can think of."[12]

"Well," said Annie, "there was my voice. My voice was louder when I was confident and very quiet when I was shy."

"That's right," said Annie's mom.

"And my shoulders were different," said Annie. "When I was confident, my shoulders were straight. When I was shy, they were slumped down."

"Yes, that's good," said her mom. "You're very good at this."

"And I know another one," Annie said. She was enjoying this. "I held my head up when I was confident and I had it down when I was shy."

"Yes," said her mom. "And another thing—you looked me in the eye when you were confident and you avoided my eyes when you were shy."

"Yes, that's right," said Annie, "I did."

"Well," said her mom, "now you know a lot of things about being confident when you go up to people. That's an excellent beginning."

"What about what I say after I go up to them?" asked Annie. "I'm always worried that I won't know what to say or that I'll sound stupid."

"What sorts of things do Janet and the other girls say to each other?" asked her mom.

Annie thought for a while. "Well," she said, "they talk about

---

If your child loves to act, make use of this in encouraging them to "act" as if they were socially confident.

[12]Breaking down body language and verbal communication into parts makes it easier for the child to come to grips with it.

TV shows and pop stars and things. They sometimes talk about teachers and assignments. They talk about what's on at the movies."

"Well," said her mom, "those are all things you know about, aren't they?"

"Yes," said Annie, "I guess so." She hadn't thought of it like that before.[13]

"So," said her mom, "what are some of the things you could say about them?"

"Well," said Annie, "I could say I think that Mr. Green's being really unfair about the math assignments. I could say I really like Samantha Starr's new poster and that her new hairdo looks great. I could say that I can't wait to see Steve Jay's new movie."[14]

"It sounds as if there are quite a few things you could talk about," said her mom.

Annie was surprised. "Yes," she said. "I guess there are."

"Something that's useful to remember," said Annie's mom, "is that most people like to be asked questions about what they think about things. It makes them feel that you're interested in them and their opinions. So you could also ask questions that would get people talking."

"You mean like ask them whether they think the math assignment is unfair?" said Annie.

"Yes," said her mom. "Then you can tell them what you think, and then you might ask them what they think of Mr. Green, and before you know it, you've got quite a conversation going."

"Gee," said Annie, "it sounds a lot easier when you say it like that."

"The other thing to remember," said Annie's mom, "is that when you're in a group of girls, you don't really need to say much at all unless you want to. You can just listen to what the others are saying. If you have any ideas, you can say them, but if you don't, you

---

[13]Often children imagine that the conversations around them are carried on at some higher plane of youthful wit and sophistication that they could never aspire to. It helps to analyze the conversations so that they can recognize that they don't have to be a talented conversationalist in order to make a contribution.

[14]Rehearsing conversational gambits can be very helpful.

don't need to. You can just say simple things like 'yes' and 'no' or 'that sounds great' in just the way the others are doing."[15]

"Oh," said Annie, "I always thought people would think I'm a dummy if I didn't talk a lot."

"Not usually," said her mom. "In any group of kids there are usually some who talk a lot and some who don't talk much. It's pretty normal. People would just think you were one of the quieter ones. They wouldn't think you were a dummy."

"Really?" said Annie. "But I feel like a dummy. I feel really stupid and ugly."[16]

"Goodness," said Annie's mom, and she gave her a hug. "That sounds like a miserable way to feel. Whatever gave you the idea that you were dumb and stupid and ugly?"

"I don't know," said Annie. "I just feel like I am."

"I've got a good idea," said Annie's mom. "Let's get out a pencil and paper and make a very special list."

"What sort of list?" asked Annie. She was curious.

"A list of the things you like about yourself and the things you don't like. Or the things that you think are good about yourself and the things that you think are bad about yourself."[17]

"All right," said Annie. She was sure she was going to be able to fill the whole page with things that were bad about herself.

Her mom took a piece of paper and ruled a line down the middle. On the left side she wrote "Good things" and on the right side she wrote "Bad things."

"Okay," said Annie, "number one, I'm stupid."

Her mom wrote down "stupid" on the bad column. Then she said, "On the other hand, you get very good grades in English, social studies, science, and art. So I think we can write 'smart' in the good column."

---

[15] It's helpful to remind shy children that they don't have to come up with lengthy monologues or fascinating dialogue to be part of a group.

[16] Shy children often have low self-esteem. It is important to build their self-esteem up. Find ways to praise them. Point out their achievements, however small, and encourage them to be proud of them.

[17] This can be a valuable exercise. Children with low self-esteem forget or don't acknowledge the fact that they have good qualities. Having them there in black and white is a positive reminder.

Annie looked at her mom. "That's weird," she said. "How can I be smart and stupid at the same time?"

"Well," said her mom, "maybe you're not really stupid."

"But I think I'm stupid," said Annie.

"What do you mean by 'stupid'?" Mom asked.[18]

"I mean things like I never know what to say to people," said Annie.

"You mean you never *ever* know what to say to people?" asked her mom. "I've heard you chatting quite comfortably to people at times."

"All right," said Annie, "I guess it's that I usually don't know what to say to people."

"Okay, then," said her mom. "Let's cross out 'stupid' and write 'Often doesn't know what to say to people.'"

"Okay," said Annie.

"I know another one for the good side," said her mom, and she wrote down "kind."

"That's true," said Annie. "I am a kind person."

"I know another one," said her mom and she wrote down "trustworthy."

Annie nodded. She was very trustworthy.

Half an hour later, Annie and her mom had finished the list. To Annie's astonishment, the good list was much longer than the bad list.

"This is weird," she said to her mom. "I never knew there were so many good things about me."

"I have a good idea," said her mom. "Why don't we put your list in a special frame? We can hang it up in your room to remind you of how many good things there are about you."

"Okay," said Annie. "I'd like that."

"You remember how I was saying that the more you practiced being confident, the easier it was to be confident?" asked Annie's mom.

---

[18]It's useful to analyze your child's sweeping negatives, for example, "Everyone hates me," "I can't do anything right," "I'm dumb." When these over-generalizations are analyzed, they invariably come down to much more manageable faults and weaknesses.

"Sure," said Annie. "I remember that."

"Well," said her mom, "there are a few different ways that you can practice being confident."

"What are they?" asked Annie.

"One of the first things you can do," said Mom, "is learn how to relax. When you're relaxed, it's much easier to feel confident."

"I definitely want to learn how to relax," said Annie.

"Okay," said her mom. "It's fun. I think you'll enjoy it." And she showed Annie how to relax.[19]

"Now that you're relaxed," said Annie's mom, "you might like to practice being confident in your imagination. It really helps you to be confident in real life."[20]

"Okay," said Annie. "How do I do it?"

Mom thought for a moment. Then she told Annie, "Imagine yourself looking confident and asking some of the kids if you can join in their game."

"What should I say to them?" asked Annie.

"What do the other kids say?" asked her mom.

Annie thought. "I guess they just say things like, 'Hi, can I join in?' or 'That looks like a good game. Can I play?.'"

"Those sound like good things to say when you want to join in," said Annie's mom. "Why don't you try saying something like that?"

So Annie did. She imagined herself, relaxed and confident, going up to some kids and saying, "Hi. Can I join in?"

"Hey," she said to her mom. "That was easier that I thought. You were right, it is easier when you're relaxed."

"Why don't you try imagining it with a different group of kids?"[21]

"Okay," said Annie and she did.

"I like doing this," she said. "I feel good when I see myself looking confident and asking kids to play."[22]

---

[19]The Relaxation story (chapter 14) covers ways of helping children relax. You might want to take a break at this point and teach your child how to relax.

[20]Practicing skills in one's imagination is a very effective aid to mastering those skills.

[21]I've focused here on playground social interactions, but you can use the same techniques to help your child deal with classroom participation and so on.

[22]Depending on your child, you might want to break this down into smaller steps.

"Why don't you imagine looking confident and going up to say hello to one of the kids you don't know very well?" said her mom.

"Okay," said Annie. And she imagined herself going up to Josie, the new girl in class, and smiling and saying, "Hi."

"That felt good," said Annie. "I might imagine myself asking her whether she's done the math assignment yet."

"That's a great idea," said her mom. "You're very good at this."

Annie was enjoying herself so much that she imagined doing all sorts of confident things.

"Now that you're getting so good at doing confident things in your imagination," said her mom, "would you like to try doing them in real life?"

"All right," said Annie, "but can I start with little things first? That way I'll feel better when I get to the big things."[23]

"That's very good thinking," said her mom. "Why don't we draw up a list of things you can do, starting with the smaller things and working up?"

"We could start with me smiling at someone," said Annie. "That could be number one on the list."

"Good idea," said her mom, and wrote that down.

"Then I could say 'Hi,'" said Annie. "That could be the next thing."

"Sounds good," said her mom.

"After that, I could ask if they'd done their math assignment yet."

"Okay," said her mom and wrote that down as number three.

Soon they had a long list of things that Annie could do.

"I have a good idea," said her mom. "Why don't we make a chart with all the days of the week on it? Start with number one on the list, smiling at someone, and write it down the side here. Then, every day when you smile at someone, you could put a star next to that day. When you have four stars, you can get a special treat."[24]

---

For instance, you could start with just making eye contact, then smiling, then saying hello and so on.

[23] It's useful to start with small steps that the child can master. This gives her a sense of achievement and confidence which in turn helps her master the next steps. You might also want to give your child practice by acting out social scenes with her.

[24] Children love star charts. They provide incentive and also a concrete reminder of achievements.

"That sounds great," said Annie. Then she said, "I already know what I want my treat to be."

"What's that?" asked her mom.

"The box of magic tricks that I saw in the shop the other day. I want to be a magician."

"Okay," said her mom. "When you've smiled at people on four days and gotten four stars, you can get your box of tricks."

"What happens if I get nervous?" asked Annie.

"If you get nervous," said her mom, "a good thing to do is to take three slow breaths and that will help you relax. You can also remind yourself that it's okay to smile at people—most people like being smiled at—and that you're an okay kid. That you're just as good as anyone else. You can remind yourself, too, that even if they don't smile back at you, it's not the end of the world. It doesn't mean that you're a terrible person, it just means that they didn't feel like smiling."[25]

"I guess you're right," said Annie. "It feels better hearing things like that. I used to feel as if it would be the worst thing in the world if I smiled at someone and they didn't smile back."

"What did you think would happen?" asked her mom.

"Well," said Annie, "I used to think they would think I was an idiot, the dumbest person on Earth."

"Well," said her mom, "that's definitely not the worst thing in the world. I can think of some worse things."

"What?" asked Annie. She was curious.

"Let's see," said her mom. "The principal might call you up to the front at assembly and say, 'Children, I just wanted you to have a look at the dumbest girl in the world.'" Annie's mom paused. "Then the newspapers might hear about it and they'd print a story with a big picture of you on the front page and underneath it would say, 'Annie—the dumbest girl in the world!'"

Annie was starting to smile. "Then the TV could pick up on it," she said. "I could be on the local news as the dumbest girl in the world."

"Yes," said her mom, "you'd never be able to walk down the street

---

[25] It's useful to give your child some brief techniques she can use to contain anxiety. The two used here are slow breathing for relaxation and positive self-talk. (See Impulsive Children, Chapter 11, for more on self-talk.)

again because everyone would be mobbing you, dying to see the dumbest girl in the world."

Annie giggled. "I might get asked for autographs," she said.

"That's right," said her mom. "It isn't every day that you get to meet a celebrity like the dumbest girl in the world. I bet you'd get on the 'Donahue Show.'"

"And 'Good Morning America,'" said Annie. She was laughing now. "I think it could be fun being the dumbest girl in the world."

"Well," said her mom, "I think the hardest part will be to convince everyone that you really are the dumbest girl in the world."[26]

Annie looked at her mom and laughed. "You mean smiling at someone wouldn't be enough to convince them that I'm the dumbest girl in the world?"

Her mom looked at Annie and laughed, too. "Somehow," she said, "I very much doubt it."

A week later Annie was looking at her chart with her mom.

"Wow," said her mom. "Five stars. You smiled at five people on different days. That's fantastic."

"It wasn't as bad as I thought it would be," said Annie. "Sometimes I even felt like laughing because I kept remembering 'Good Morning America' and the evening news."

Her mom gave her a hug. "Tonight we'll get your box of magic tricks," she said. "But before we do, why don't we make a chart for next week? This time the stars will be for saying hello."

"Great," said Annie. She was enjoying this. "Can I make the chart myself?"

"You sure can," said her mom. She gave Annie a big smile. "I'm really proud of you."

A few weeks later, Annie came home from school very excited. "Mom, Mom, the best thing happened!" she said. "We had to talk in front of the class about our favorite hobby. I took my magic box and did some magic tricks, and everyone loved it. All the kids have been asking me to show them how to do tricks. They all want to talk to me.

---

[26]Humor and hyperbole can defuse anxiety and add perspective.

They all said my tricks are really neat and that I do them like a real magician. I had such a great time!"[27]

"Wow!" said Annie's mom and she gave Annie a hug. "I'm really proud of you."

"Me, too," said Annie. And she smiled a great big smile.

---

[27]Having a special skill like this can be a useful "ice-breaker" with children just as it can with adults.

# 8

## Teasing

Most of us have been teased at one time or another. Often it has been done warmly, in the context of an enjoyable, easy intimacy. We laugh with the teaser and don't feel put down at all. At other times, however, the teasing is meant to make us feel uncomfortable. It's intended to make us feel put down, to make us blush or squirm. In these instances, teasing is clearly an unpleasant experience. Usually it doesn't go on for long and we can simply shrug it off. However, if teasing becomes a pattern or is difficult to shrug off, then it's time to do something about it. This chapter is aimed at children in this position.

Children who are the butt of constant teasing feel miserable. Their self-esteem is often low, they feel humiliated and shamed in front of their peers. They feel angry, hurt, and powerless. If the teasing becomes a pattern, a vicious circle begins in which the more they are teased, the more powerless and inadequate they feel, and the more they are likely to be teased. It is important to reverse this cycle if the teasing is to be stopped. In this Annie Story, Annie's mother teaches Annie how to be a behavioral scientist. This does several things. It makes Annie feel special and important. It engages her interest and it puts her in control. As a behavioral scientist, she is conducting the experiment, and the teaser becomes the experimental rat in the cage. This, of course, is a complete reversal of the previous roles of teaser and teased.

It is also helpful to teach children about body language—some children cringe along, almost carrying a placard that says "Please Tease Me." Body language is discussed in more detail in the Annie

Story on shyness. Teaching children to relax (see Relaxation, Chapter 14) can also help. While they're relaxed, you can encourage them to imagine themselves being teased and not being fazed by the experience. You can also teach children to think to themselves, "She's only doing this to make me react" or "She's only doing this because she's not smart enough to get a laugh any other way." Another good method is to act out the roles of teaser and teased so that your child gets practice at not responding to teasing (see Impulsive Children, Chapter 11).

## annie story

Annie was a little girl who lived in a brown brick house with her mommy and her daddy and a big black dog.[1]

Annie went to a nearby school. Annie mostly liked school. She liked Miss Matson, her teacher. She liked doing drawings. She liked learning about things. She liked playing games. She liked seeing her friends. But there was one thing Annie didn't like about school, and that was Mary.

Mary had come to Annie's school a few months ago and had been put into Annie's class. At first, Mary hadn't paid much attention to Annie, but lately Mary had paid a lot of attention to her. And Annie wished she wouldn't. That was because Mary had started to tease Annie. Every time Mary saw Annie, in fact, she would tease her. She would call her names and make up nasty rhymes about her. She would make jokes about Annie, and she and her friends would laugh at Annie.

Annie hated it. She would get all hot and bothered and feel like crying. Sometimes she would cry. She would hang her head down low and hope that if she crept by and didn't look at Mary, Mary wouldn't tease her. But Mary teased her anyway. Annie tried to avoid Mary, but Mary always found her. The more Annie blushed and hung her head and looked as if she were about to burst into

---

[1]Change the details to suit your child.

tears, the more Mary laughed and the more Mary teased.[2] Annie wished she were invisible. She wished she didn't have to go to school. She wished she didn't have to be Annie.

One day, Annie came home from school particularly upset. Her mom saw her and gave her a hug.

"You haven't been very happy lately," her mom said.

Annie looked up miserably. "I hate school," she said.

"But you used to like school," said Annie's mom. "What happened? Is something upsetting you at school?"

Annie nodded.

"Is it a problem with the teacher?" asked her mom.

Annie shook her head.

"Is it the schoolwork?" asked her mom.

Annie shook her head.

"Is it the kids?" asked her mom.

Annie nodded. "It's Mary," she said. "She's always teasing me. She calls me names and tries to make people laugh at me. She makes fun of me. I hate her."

Annie's mom gave her another hug. "That must be awful for you," she said.

"She won't stop," said Annie. She was starting to cry a little bit. "She goes on and on. She just teases and teases, and she won't stop." Annie gave a big sniff. "I hate it, but she won't stop and there's nothing I can do."[3]

"You must be feeling terrible," said Annie's mom, "especially when you think there's nothing you can do."

Annie nodded unhappily.

"But you're wrong," said her mom, "because there is something you can do. Quite a few things, actually."

"Really?" said Annie. She was surprised. "You mean there's really something I can do?"[4]

"There certainly is," said her mom.

---

[2]This is the classic vicious cycle. The more the person being teased responds like this to the teasing, the more she is likely to be teased.

[3]Many children feel helpless and impotent in the face of teasing.

[4]This restores a feeling of power and confidence.

"Oh, wow," said Annie. "That would be great!" She was beginning to feel better already.

"Come and sit down in the kitchen," said her mom. "We have to make plans. We're going to turn you into a junior behavioral scientist."

"A what?" asked Annie. She had never heard of a junior whatever-it-was, but it sounded impressive.

"A junior behavioral scientist," said her mom. "A scientist is a very important person who studies the way things work. A behavioral scientist studies the way people work. Why they do the things they do and how to stop them from acting that way, for instance."

"Oh," said Annie. She was beginning to see that being a junior behavioral scientist could be very useful as well as important.[5] "How do I begin?"

"Well," said her mom, "do you remember when Blackie was a puppy and we had to train her not to do her doggy-doos in the house?"

"I remember that," said Annie.

"We knew that puppies usually do their doggy-doos right after a meal. So we'd feed her and watch her and when she looked as if she was just about to do one, we'd rush her out into the backyard and give her lots of pats and say 'good dog' when she did it there. After a while, she had learned to do her doggy-doos in the backyard and not in the house."

"I remember that," said Annie. "Were you being a behavioral scientist with Blackie?"[6]

"You're absolutely right," said her mom. "She was doing something we didn't want her to do, so we worked out how to change her behavior."

"Hey, that's neat," said Annie. "I never thought of it like that before."

"As behavioral scientists," said her mom, "there were a few other things we could have tried to stop her from doing doggy-

---

[5]This puts Annie in a position of power and authority as opposed to the position of victim.

[6]Everyday examples will help your child understand the principles.

doos in the house. We could have waited until she'd done some and smacked her and put her outside, for instance."

"If there are a few things you can do, how do you decide which one to do?" asked Annie.

"Well, a real behavioral scientist would try each thing in turn, see which one worked best, and then use that as his training method. We could have done that with Blackie, but the first method worked so well that we didn't have to try any others."

"How would I start training Mary?" asked Annie. She was beginning to get quite excited.

"Well," said her mom, "why don't we sit down and think of a few different ways of training Mary? Then you can be a junior behavioral scientist and test them out to see which one works best."

"Goody," said Annie. This sounded like it was going to be fun.

"First of all," said her mom, "we know one method that doesn't work."

"What's that?" asked Annie, puzzled.

"Think about it," said her mom with a smile.

Annie thought for a few moments and then her face brightened. "I know," she said. "It's what I do now. That doesn't work because Mary keeps on teasing me. It doesn't change her behavior."[7]

"That's right," said her mom. "I can see you're going to make an excellent JBS."

"JBS?" said Annie. Then she laughed. "You mean Junior Behavioral Scientist."

"That's right," said her mom.

"I'm going to be a great JBS," said Annie. She was looking forward to it.

"Okay," said her mom. "Let's begin." She got a piece of paper and made three columns. Over the first column she wrote, "What Mary did." Over the second she wrote, "What Annie did." And over the third she wrote, "What happened."

"Now," she said, "let's fill in what we already know."

---

[7]A lot of us fall into the trap of blindly repeating patterns of behavior even when they don't work.

In the first column, "What Mary did," Mom wrote "Mary teased Annie." In the second column, "What Annie did," she said to Annie, "What will we write here?"

"Well," said Annie, "when Mary teased me I got upset and cried."

So her mom wrote, "Annie got upset and cried."

"Now," she said, "what happened after you got upset and cried?"

"Mary kept on teasing," said Annie.

So her mom wrote in the third column, "Mary kept teasing."

"Okay," she said. "Now let's think of some other things you could have done."

Annie thought. "I could have pretended I didn't care and not paid any attention to what she said."

"That's a good one," said Annie's mom.

She got out another piece of paper and wrote, "Things to try out" on it. Then she wrote down "1. Pretend not to notice."

"What's another thing you could have done?" she asked.

"I could have pretended I thought it was funny and laughed," said Annie.

"Yes," said her mom and wrote that down as number 2.

"I could have made a face at her," said Annie. "That could be number 3."

"Right," said her mom and wrote it down.

"I could have teased her back," said Annie. She was beginning to get lots of ideas now. "I could have told her she was being silly and to stop doing it."

"They can be numbers 4 and 5," said her mom.

"I could have told her that I didn't like being teased and asked her why she was doing it."

"Great," said her mom. "That makes six things you could do."

"Wow!" said Annie. She hadn't realized there were so many things she could do.

"Now," said her mom, "we need to work out the order you'll try them out in."

"Why not make it the same order that I thought them up?" Annie asked.

"Okay," said her mom, "we can do that."

"When do I start?" asked Annie. She was eager to get going with this.

"Well, the first thing you have to do is figure out how much Mary teases you now. That way you can see whether what you do makes her tease you more or less or the same. That's what JBSs call establishing a baseline."

"Okay," said Annie. "How do I establish a baseline?" She felt good using such an important scientific word. She was going to be a terrific JBS.

"Well," said her mom, "you take a little notebook with you to school and every time Mary teases you, you make a check mark in it. You do it for two weeks on every school day. Then we can find out the average number of times a day Mary teases you, and that number will be our baseline.[8] In that two weeks you have to have ten school days. So if you have a school holiday, or Mary isn't at school one day, you do it for an extra day until you have ten."

"That sounds easy," said Annie. "I'll start tomorrow."

Two weeks later, she showed her notebook to her mother. "Look," she said, "I've got ten days and twenty marks in my book."

"Good work," said her mom. "You've got your baseline now. That means Mary teases you about twice a day on average."

"You know something funny?" said Annie thoughtfully. "I was so busy getting my baseline that Mary's teasing didn't bother me as much as before."

"That's very interesting," said her mom. "Let's have a look at your notebook."

Annie pointed to her notebook. "I made a space for every day," she said, "and I marked down how many times Mary teased me each day."

"Look at the difference between week one and week two," said her mom.

---

[8]To get the average number of times Mary teases Annie, divide the total number of check marks by the number of days. This will give you a baseline to compare future results with.

Annie looked. "Hey," she said. "Mary didn't tease me as much in the second week. That's funny."

"Let's think about it," said her mom. "You said that you didn't get as upset as you used to over Mary's teasing. Maybe the fact that you're not getting as upset is changing Mary's behavior?"

"I bet you're right," said Annie. She thought for a moment. Then she said, "If my not getting upset changes Mary's behavior, maybe not paying any attention at all would change it even more. Hey, isn't it lucky that I'm trying not-paying-any-attention first."

"It is very handy," said her mom.

"Great," said Annie. "I'll start it tomorrow."

"Good idea," said her mom. "But before you start, there's a little extra something that will be helpful to know."

"What's that?" asked Annie.

"Well," said her mom, "why do you think Mary teases you?" Annie thought for a minute. "To get me upset?" she said.

"Yes," said her mom. "People often tease because they like to get people upset. So, if you get upset, then Mary gets what she wants, and she knows that teasing works on you."

"Oh," said Annie. "You mean that whenever she wants to get me upset, she knows that all she has to do is tease me?"

"That's exactly right," said her mom. "Remember what Blackie does when she wants a dog biscuit?"

"She sits up and begs," said Annie.

"Yes," said her mom, "and then we give it to her."

Annie nodded.

"What do you think would happen," said her mom, "if we stopped giving her a dog biscuit when she begged?"

Annie thought. "She'd stop begging," she said, "because she'd know it wouldn't work."

"Exactly," said her mom. "Good thinking, JBS." She paused. "Now, what do you think would happen if sometimes when Blackie begged, we gave her a biscuit, and sometimes we didn't?"

Annie thought for a while. "I think she'd keep begging," she said. "Because if we kept giving her biscuits every now and then, she'd think it was still working."

"That's quite right," said Annie's mom. "So, as a JBS, when you test the not-paying-any-attention method, you have to do it every single time Mary teases you. Otherwise she might think that teasing still works."[9]

"That makes sense," said Annie. "I think I can do that."

"If you make a mistake, we just start over again, because we have to do it for ten school days in a row. It just means it takes a little longer if you make a mistake."

"That's good," said Annie. Now she didn't have to be nervous about making a mistake.

"Now," said her mom. "What do you look like when you're upset by Mary's teasing?"

"Well," said Annie, "I go like this." And she hung her head and drooped her shoulders and tried to get red-faced and teary.

"Okay," said her mom. "Now, to show Mary that teasing doesn't work and that you're not getting upset, we have to practice doing the opposite of what you do when you get upset."

"Oh, I see," said Annie. "You mean like this." And she straightened her shoulders and held her head up proudly.[10]

"That's great," said Annie's mom. "Tell you what, why don't we practice this? I'll pretend to be Mary and tease you and you can ignore me."

"Okay," said Annie.

So Annie's mom pretended to be Mary.[11] She called out mean things to Annie and stuck out her tongue but Annie didn't pay any attention at all. She just walked straight past.

"Silly Mary's trying to get me upset," Annie thought to herself. "But I'm the JBS around here and I'm not going to pay any attention to her."[12]

"That's terrific," said Annie's mom. "You're very good at this." She gave Annie a hug. "Now you're all set to go."

Annie was very excited. She was really looking forward to tomorrow.

---

[9]Whenever you're trying to change someone's behavior, consistency is very important.
[10]Body language is very important in communicating (see Shyness, Chapter 7).
[11]Role playing helps children practice their new responses in a safe setting.
[12]"Self-talk" can help keep children calm and focused on their goals. For more on self-talk, see Impulsive Children, Chapter 11.

The next day at school, Annie couldn't wait for Mary to tease her so she could try out looking-confident and not-paying-any-attention.

Annie had to wait quite a while before Mary teased her, but finally she did.

Annie didn't pay any attention at all.

"This is great," she said to her mom when she got home that day. "This is really fun."

"You did a great job today," said her mom. "You're a real JBS now."

Annie was very pleased. "Every time Mary teases me," she said, "I'm going to look confident and not pay any attention. I'm going to do it every single time."

"Terrific," said her mom. "I can't wait to see what happens."

"Me neither," said Annie.

Nine days later, Annie came to her mother and put on a very worried face. "I have a problem, Mom," she said. "I can't not-pay-attention to Mary's teasing anymore."

"Why not?" asked her mom, looking concerned.

"Because she stopped teasing me!" said Annie and burst out laughing. "She hasn't teased me for four whole days!"

"Wow!" said her mom. "Not-paying-any-attention really worked well."

"Yes," said Annie. "It worked so well that I don't think I'll bother with the other methods. I'll just keep on not-paying-any-attention."

"That's a good idea," said her mom. "I'm very proud of my JBS."

"And you know what?" said Annie. "I've decided what I'm going to be when I grow up."

"What?" said her mom.

"I'm going to be a SBS," said Annie.

"What's that?" said her mom.

"A Senior Behavioral Scientist," said Annie, and they both burst out laughing.

# 2
# Divorce

Divorce is an enormously complicated subject. Everyone's divorce is different, and yet if you got a roomful of people to compare notes on how divorce affected them, you would find that much of the roomful was bobbing up and down with the nods of recognition that signify, "Yes, I felt like that too!"

It would be impossible to write an Annie Story that encompasses all the variations upon the divorce theme. So instead, I have devoted some extra space to sketching out information about divorce and children's reactions to it for you to draw on when making up your own Annie Story.

Divorce, of course, is becoming increasingly common in our society. Although it has lost some of its old shock-horror value, it nevertheless usually manages to bring in its wake a bundle of assorted sorrows that the thirteenth fairy or some other malevolent spirit would be proud to call her own.

Divorce places a huge stress on everyone concerned with it. People react with a multitude of emotions—rage, guilt, sadness, fear, relief, yearning, and so on. Although divorce is highly traumatic for most children, research suggests that in the long term it need not necessarily lead to lasting emotional damage. It is the background of the divorce that generally affects how well a child recovers from this painful event. I'll be discussing the factors that make up this background in the following sections.

## Children's Reactions to Divorce

Most children show signs of stress in the first year or so following a separation or divorce. Anger, sadness, and confusion are chief among the emotions they tend to experience.

Children may be angry at either or both parents for not keeping the family together. They may be angry at themselves, feeling that their naughtiness drove mom and dad apart or that they failed to do something that would have kept the parents together. These angry feelings may be difficult for the child to handle and express. She may fear, for instance, that if she shows her anger to the noncustodial parent, she may be rejected entirely and lose her visiting times. Similarly, she may imagine that if she gets too angry at the parent she is living with, this parent may reject her as well. She may be scared by the intensity of her anger, fearing that if she lets even some of it out, it will become uncontrollable.

Anger about one parent may also be redirected onto another parent with whom it is safer to feel angry. This is something we all do. Think back to the times we've had outbursts of anger at old friends or relatives we know won't desert us. With new friends or more precarious relatives, we might have held the anger back, scared that if we made a wrong move, they'd be off and running. It's a sort of compliment, really, to feel that someone is safe enough to get angry with—although that rarely helps when you're on the receiving end of the anger.

Sometimes the child's anger may spill out onto school friends and teachers or be displayed in destructive, acting-out behavior. This is the "kick the cat" phenomenon, typified by the business woman who comes home furious after being told off by her boss. She can't kick the boss or she'll be fired so she lets out her anger on the nearest moving object—the hapless cat.

Sadness is an almost universal accompaniment to divorce. It is natural to feel sad about such a painful loss, and children as well as adults have to go through the process of mourning the breakup of their family.

Coupled with the sadness may be feelings of inadequacy and low self-esteem. The child may feel she is worthless, bad, or unlovable. She may feel that she can't do anything right.

Sometimes a child's sadness may take the form of a passive withdrawal from life. She may mope around and be uninterested in school, her friends, or any of the other things she used to enjoy.

Sometimes there is a frenzy of agitated overactivity, as if the child is trying to run away from the sad feelings.

The child may be weepy, crying at things that never used to upset her, redeveloping fears, such as that of the dark, that she had previously mastered, or developing new ones. If she has been toilet-trained, she may regress to wetting herself. She may demand extra attention and find normal, everyday separations, such as going to school, hard to tolerate. She may develop physical symptoms such as tummyaches or have problems concentrating in school.

In the chaos of a divorce, it is also common for the child to feel lost and forgotten. Often the parents find it difficult to deal with their own overwhelming feelings and have little emotional energy to spare for her. This is very frightening for her, and she may frantically redouble her attempts to get attention and end up being perceived as whining or naughty.

She often feels confused as well, prey to conflicting feelings. Sometimes she feels relieved that the fighting will end when daddy moves out, and at the same time she may desperately wish that he would stay. It is hard for her to look into the future and comprehend the finality of divorce. Young children have trouble comprehending next week, let alone next month or next year. She may be confused about what caused the divorce and what her new relationship with her parents will be. She may feel torn between her parents, alternately angry and pleading, not sure who, if anyone, is to blame. She may wonder about how or whether to tell her friends, her teachers, and the other people in her life. Overall, she is also likely to feel painfully and frighteningly helpless. Here is probably the most excruciating and overwhelming event of her life and there is not a thing she can do about it.

## Children's Fears and Fantasies

Perhaps the primary fear experienced by the child going through a divorce is that of abandonment. If we think back to childhood, most of us can remember the dread we felt on some occasion when, for instance, we lost sight of Mommy in the supermarket. We stood there, filled with the sheer cold terror, the sickening emptiness, of being little, lost, and horribly alone. This fear of abandonment is common even in children of intact families. It has to do with the child's innate helplessness and dependence on her parents. Fairy tales from all over the world feature this theme of abandonment; "Hansel and Gretel" is a prime example.

With divorce, all of the child's fantasies about being abandoned may seem to be coming true. It is very important to reassure your child that she will not be abandoned. This reassurance will most likely need to be repeated frequently. Everyday situations such as being left with a babysitter may rekindle the fear that you are never coming back. Sometimes telling your child where you are going and leaving a number where she can phone you can be reassuring.

Children sometimes believe that they were to blame for the divorce. A child may feel that her naughtiness drove Daddy away from the house. Or she may feel that Mommy and Daddy split up because they were arguing so much about her bad behavior. This belief that they have caused events reflects children's sense of their omnipotence. When we're little, we believe the world revolves around us and all the things that happen in it are affected by us. Most of us, as we grow up, are rather sorrowfully forced to discard this regal outlook and come to terms with our real relative place in the scheme of things.

In some families, of course, the child's fear of being the cause of divorce is tremendously reinforced when the parent, in fact, blames the child or children for the divorce. To tell your child that she was responsible for your divorce is to put an intolerable burden on her and should never be done.

Young children also exhibit what psychologists call "magical thinking." This involves the belief that thoughts or feelings can actually cause things to happen in the physical world. The child who has felt angry at a parent after being punished, for instance, may believe that her angry thoughts caused the parent to trip on the staircase or to become ill or to separate from the family.

"How silly!" you may exclaim, secure in your adult wisdom. But think about it the next time you avoid walking under a ladder or touch wood for luck. Magical thinking isn't that far away from most of us.

Parallel to the feeling that something she did drove her parents apart is the equally common fantasy that somehow the child can do something to bring her parents back together again. A great many children try all sorts of tactics to reunite their family. The little girl may think that if she is very good, Daddy will come home again. Or that if she is very bad, the parents will need to get together to consult with each other about her behavior. She may feel that if she were sick, Daddy would have to come home again.

Children almost invariably hold on to the fantasy that their mother and father will get back together again for a long time after the divorce has become final.

Children fear not only for their own welfare, but for that of their parents. They may worry about "poor Daddy" alone in his apartment and having to look after himself. Or they may worry about Mommy, who is looking so sad and tired. They may worry about financial matters—such worries are fueled by parents' comments such as "She's taken every last cent from me" and "We're never going to be able to live on the money he's giving us."

Children often fantasize about an absent parent. They may build up such an idealized image of a parent they see only infrequently that the real thing is bound to be a crashing disappointment.

Sometimes the weaker and more inadequate a parent is, the more the child idealizes him or her. This is because it would be too painful for the child to acknowledge how pitiful or inadequate her father, for instance, really is; instead, she builds up a fantasy picture. On the other hand, it is easy to acknowledge the faults of a competent parent because the child knows that even with a few faults, the parent is good enough and solid enough to love, look up to, and rely on.

These fears and fantasies are common to many children, but it is a good idea to ask your own child what her fears are about divorce. Even if she can't readily verbalize them, perhaps she can draw them or paint them.

## How to Tell Children

Whenever possible, break the news about the upcoming separation to your child before you or your spouse has actually moved out. This will give her time to think about the news, get over some of the initial shock, and talk to both of you about what it all means for her. Children need to have repeated opportunities with both parents to ask questions and talk about their feelings. They need time to digest the new situation and come back to it. Don't expect that just one heart-to-heart talk will take care of everything.

Sometimes it is difficult for children to express their feelings verbally. It's always a good idea to encourage them to let their thoughts and feelings out through artwork, puppet-play or storytelling. Children's artwork gives a wonderful glimpse into their inner thoughts and feelings.

When you're explaining divorce to your child, make sure that your explanation is phrased in terms your child can understand. Research has shown that a surprising number of children were either not given an explanation of the divorce or given one that was above their heads. Children who were given an explanation they could understand fared much better emotionally than those who were not. Children who are left in the dark about divorce are often forced into a desperate search for clues and meanings in their efforts to make sense of the world they now find themselves in.

It is important, too, that the explanations you give your children are appropriate to their age group. It is not appropriate, for instance, to flood an eight-year-old girl with details of daddy's affairs.

Be aware that children will need different levels of information as they get older. As the ten-year-old becomes a twelve-year-old, for instance, she will have more awareness of how adult relationships function and may want to know, and be able to understand, more about the complexities of your divorce. It's important to remember that divorce is a process in a family's life, not a single discrete event.

When talking to your child about divorce, be sure to stress that while marriage partners can divorce each other, parents cannot divorce children. Make it clear that you will always be their parent and be there to take care of them. For the noncustodial parent who has visitation rights and expectations, it is important to stress that even though you won't be living with your child, you still love her and are still her mother or father and she will always be a part of your life. Don't make these promises, however, if you don't fully intend to keep them. Broken promises of this kind are truly heartbreaking for children.

When a parent has deserted or does not want contact with a child, it is important to let the child know that the problem lies within that parent. Children often think that their badness or worthlessness is the cause of a parent deserting them. Stress to your child that the deserting parent was simply not grown-up enough to be a parent or had too many problems to be able to parent properly. Bolster your child's self-esteem and reassure her about her worth and value.

In general, when telling a child about your impending separation or divorce, let her know that it is not her fault. She did nothing to cause it, could have done nothing to prevent it, and cannot bring you back together again. Divorce is a decision made by adults, not children. Also stress the finality of the divorce. Children often maintain the fantasy that parents will reunite for a very long time after the divorce. It is best not to encourage that fantasy.

When you talk to your child about divorce, acknowledge that it is a difficult process to get through but that you will make it. Too often parents tell children, "Things will be better after the divorce," when in fact it usually takes some time for the expected improvement to take place. Children then become confused and mistrustful on seeing that things are in fact worse immediately after the divorce.

Finally, make sure your child understands your explanations. Just because your daughter can parrot you by saying "Mommy and Daddy are getting a divorce" does not mean that she understands the meaning of a divorce. Make yourself available for repeated questions. Children need to come back time and time again to this subject. They may ask different questions or they may ask the same question many times. They are not trying to be a nuisance; they are trying to grapple with an enormous upheaval in their lives and they need time, thought, information, and repeated reassurances to help them through it.

## Problems and Pitfalls

One of the major pitfalls of divorce for the child is that it is such an overwhelming and painful time for the parents that they may have little emotional energy left over for her. The child may feel abandoned by both parents not just the one who is leaving the family home. In addition, the custodial parent may have to take on extra work for financial reasons, which leaves even less time and energy for the child.

Divorcing parents often find themselves falling into the compelling, but killing, trap of competing for the child's affection and loyalty. They may engage in a battle to try and make the child choose between them. Such competition may arise out of a need to bolster their own self-esteem, out of a desire for revenge on the spouse, out of a need to see the spouse as bad, or to see the necessity for the divorce validated by the child's recoil from the ex-partner. There are many reasons why parents compete against each other in this arena but only one inevitable conclusion—the child will be severely disturbed and traumatized by this excruciating battle.

Sometimes, in an effort to win the child's approval, the non-custodial parent showers her with presents and attempts to make every moment of her visit an exciting, fun-filled extravaganza. Often, underneath this orgy of fun and present-giving is the fear that without it the parent would be rejected. Sometimes it masks the fact that the parent feels unable to communicate comfortably with the child and so enters into a frenzy of doing rather than simply being. Although children love presents and circuses, in the end what they usually crave most is simple, ordinary time with you. A time when they can tell you what happened at school, for instance, as you companionably wash the dinner dishes together.

Two distressing roles that children are often forced into during the divorce and postdivorce period are spy and message carrier.

They may be subjected to intense questioning on returning from a visit to one parent; they may be asked to keep one parent's secrets from the other or to relay messages that should more appropriately be conveyed by the parents to each other. These roles are distressing for children. In the beginning, the heightened intimacy of being the secret-keeper or the power of being the messenger may be enticing, but finally the continual shifting of loyalties can lead to an unbearably painful situation. It is too much of a load for a healthy adult to carry, let alone a vulnerable child.

Children may also attempt to manipulate parents, perhaps by playing one off against the other, sometimes with constant nudging and prodding to see how far they can go with one or other parent. This is generally the child's attempt to test the limits of her new situation. How much can she get away with before she is brought back into line? Although children can enjoy the power they feel as successful manipulators, it can also leave them feeling very insecure. If their parents aren't strong enough to control them, how can they be strong enough to be looked up to as guides, models, and protectors in a tough adult world? Children feel much more secure with firm, reasonable limit-setting. They aren't adults yet—they need parents to lay down appropriate rules and see that they are adhered to. So, though it may look as if their hearts' desire is to live in an anarchist's paradise as they attempt to break rule after rule, most children are simply seeking the relief of a solid adult force that will contain and protect them. Discipline is a common problem in the postdivorce period.

Children may have difficulty in expressing some of their emotions during this period. Sometimes, as mentioned previously, their anger at one parent can spill out onto the other or onto some unrelated person or event. Visiting times often bring conflicting emotions, and the transition from one parent to the other is usually a particularly delicate time for the child. She may have been looking forward to the visit for days with mounting and sometimes painful excitement. Yet when the day comes, she may suddenly fear leaving the custodial parent. What if Mommy isn't there when she comes back? What if Mommy gets sick while she is away or is sad and lonely without her? What if she herself gets scared in the unfamiliar surroundings of Daddy's new apartment? and so on. Parents, too, may feel mixed emotions. The custodial parent may be glad of the respite from childcaring and yet be sad or worried to see her child go. The noncustodial parent may be confused or hurt to see the child holding back and, to his eyes, obviously hedging about the visit.

Sometimes in the aftermath of a divorce, children get turned into little parents. The child may become her parent's prime confidante and source of emotional support. This is an inappropriate role for a child and one that is not helpful for her. Sometimes the child ends up taking too much responsibility for household tasks or may take on the role of parent to her younger siblings. While there is obviously a great deal more work and responsibility to be shared in a single-parent household, it is important too to give children time to be children.

One of the traps of the divorce period seems to be loaded against little boys. All children will have increased dependency needs during this period—they may need extra cuddling and reassurance, be weepy or clingy. Researchers have shown that girls tend to have their dependency needs met more satisfactorily than boys. Parents don't tend to cuddle boys as much and are less tolerant of such signs of dependency as clinging or crying. You won't spoil your children by fussing over them and meeting their needs for extra attention during this period. You'll simply make them feel more secure and therefore more able to get through this difficult time.

## What You Can Do to Make it Easier

Perhaps the most important thing you can do for your child during this period is to give her permission to be close to both of her parents. Don't force her to choose between you or make her feel she is disloyal to you when she responds positively to her other parent. Most children want a continued, close relationship with both parents. Most children love both parents despite their faults. The most loving thing you can do for your child is to recognize that she has her own feelings about your ex-spouse and that they do not have to coincide with yours.

Fathers often feel on the outside during this time if they are non-custodial parents. They may feel that their weekly visits, for instance, are not of much importance compared with the number of hours the child spends with her mother. Researchers have shown, however, that these visits, and the continued contact with the father that they represent, are extremely valuable to children and play an important part in their healthy emotional adjustment. Sadly, it is common for the frequency and predictability of visits to taper off after a few years. Children generally react to this loss with feelings of intense pain and sadness, often masked by a pose of indifference or anger.

The transition times between visits are, as I've mentioned, often times of extra stress for the child. You can help by letting her know that she is free to enjoy her time with Daddy without your being hurt or upset by it. Don't ask her to spy on Daddy or keep secrets from him. Don't recreate the Spanish Inquisition each time she comes home from a visit. Reassure her that you will be fine while she's away and that you will be there to welcome her home again. Plan a quiet day for her first day back at your home—she may need time and space to settle down and cope with the transition.

Ordinary everyday partings—going to school, visiting a friend's house—may become difficult for your child at this time. This reflects her increased insecurity and the fear of abandonment that usually surfaces with these crises. Lots of reassurance is in order about the fact that you would never abandon her, will always come back to pick her up, and so on. Giving her a special object of yours to look after for you while you're away can sometimes be helpful. It provides a link with you and also a concrete reassurance that you will be coming back.

During a divorce, children are likely to exhibit signs of stress. They may have difficulty in concentrating at school; they may become clumsy on the sportsfield and lose their place on the team; they may be grouchy with their friends or develop fears or phobias. If this happens, it is helpful to talk to your child about the way stress affects our ability to concentrate or to feel energetic and confident. Reassure her that her fading concentration doesn't mean that she's stupid, that her clumsiness doesn't mean she's a klutz, and that her fears don't mean that she's a baby.

Let her know that lots of children feel and do these things in times of stress. Most of us can remember stressful times when we behaved in such out-of-character ways that we thought we were "going crazy." What a relief it was to find that we were simply exhibiting signs of stress and not lunacy or some peculiar degenerative disease.

It can be helpful, too, if your child is tense, to teach her how to relax. For more information on this, see Chapter 14 on relaxation.

Let your child's teachers know about the divorce so that they can understand if your child's behavior at school changes. They may be able to give your child some extra support during this time.

During and following a divorce, the custodial parent often finds herself spinning frantically in a whirlpool of extra work. If it is the mother, she may have to take on new or extra work to make up for the drop in her financial status. Added to her extra working hours is the worry, strain, and general emotional drain experienced by those going through a divorce. This means that at a time when the child needs more of you, she is actually getting less of you. It can seem that each time you draw breath, your child is asking or wanting something of you. As you try to do several dozen things at once as well as field your child's requests for attention, it is easy to degenerate into something resembling the Wicked Witch of the West. One way of alleviating this situation is to set aside some special time for just you and your child, say a half-hour every evening. This is a time when you can simply sit with your child, read stories, play games, talk about the day, and, most important of all, nourish your child's self-esteem. Hug her, kiss her, talk about her special talents, how proud you are of her, and so on. Let this be a time for really letting your child feel loved and appreciated.

This sort of time makes a difference to children—after all, imagine how good you'd feel if someone did that for you every day! And because they are getting this special gift of your undivided, loving attention, they will feel much more nourished and secure and will have less need for your constant attention at other times of the day.

At this emotionally chaotic time in their lives, children particularly appreciate a secure, predictable home routine. Try to change
as few things in their life as possible. If you can, keep them at the
same school, in the same neighborhood, house, and so on. Let
them know well ahead of time when they'll be visiting Dad and
for how long. A structured, familiar routine will give them an extra
sense of security at a time when they are likely to be feeling very
insecure.

If you are moving, bring along familiar items of your own to put
in the new home. Also, if possible, allow your child to help pick
out something for the new home—perhaps a piece of furniture,
an ornament, or the color of her bedroom curtains.

This piece of advice holds true for the noncustodial parent, too.
Your new home will seem very strange to your child at first. If you
let her help decorate her room or her corner, it will help her feel
more at home.

Discipline is one of the things that often goes haywire after a
divorce. Unfortunately, discipline, in its fair, consistent, and stable
form, is one of the things that children, and particularly children
in chaos, need most. There are many reasons why discipline tends
to dissolve in divorced families. Sometimes it's because the father
has been the disciplinarian in the family. In his absence, the
mother may be struggling with a new and unfamiliar role.
Sometimes the father, in his new role as noncustodial parent, stops
disciplining the child for fear the child will reject him or because
he wants to win extra favor with the child. Often both parents are
so preoccupied with their own problems that discipline becomes
a very on-and-off affair. Sometimes they let the child do things she
normally wouldn't be allowed to get away with as a sort of com-
pensation for the divorce or because they cannot tolerate their
child's disapproval or tears.

Children at this stage often seem to be opposing discipline in
any way they can—breaking the rules, being naughty, fresh, defi-
ant. Sometimes this is their way of letting out the anger they feel
about the divorce. Often it is a way of testing the limits—seeing
how far they can go before a parent really rejects them, for
instance, or finding out how securely in control their parent really

is. The best thing you can do is reassure your child that you are committed to loving and looking after her no matter how naughty she may be at times. Many children are secretly convinced that just one more fight will make you divorce them, too. They may feel compelled to check this out in a very practical way by taking it to the limit. This motivation, though common, is not necessarily something that they can verbalize to you or understand at a conscious level.

It is imperative that while you reassure your children of your commitment to and love for them, you let them know that you will not let them run wild and that rules need to be followed. Consistent, reasonable, and caring discipline is a wonderful gift to a child. It gives her a great sense of security as well as enabling her to learn skills, such as self-control, that will aid her along the path to maturity. The extremes of disciplinary style—the harsh authoritarian style and the too soft or inconsistent permissive style—have been shown not to work as well as the middle-ground—the authoritative style, that is affectionate, has reasonable and consistent rules, and allows the child some input and explanation.

If the style of discipline at your house is different from the style at your spouse's or your parents', don't worry too much. Children will adjust to whatever household they're in, though obviously the household where they spend the most time will have the most impact on them.

Sometimes in the round of weekday mother and weekend father, the parents' roles seem to get crystallized into "goodies" and "baddies." Mom gets cast as the nagging no-sayer, while Dad gets to be the holiday-fun father. If you find yourself in this hole, with weekdays a continual round of nagging, screaming, and saying no, it's worth reevaluating things. Make sure there is time left for some loving and fun in your weekly routine. Look at the way you've been handling discipline—if it's not effective, seek some help. There are some excellent books available or, if you feel you need more, talk to a counselor or family therapist. Talk to your children about what's going on. Tell them how you're feeling, and find out how they're feeling. See if together you can work out ways of living more cooperatively and supportively with each other. Remember to praise them when they're doing the right thing. Too often we just focus on the negative behavior of our children and ignore the positive. Think about your own and your children's emotional state—is one or more of you really depressed, for instance? If so, seek professional help; you don't have to tough it out all on your own.

Finally, realize that recovery from a divorce takes time. It is foolish to expect that everyone will be perfectly adjusted to the new situation from day one. Each member of the family is bound to go through emotional ups and downs for some time as he or she works through the trauma, pain, and confusion to the eventual resolution.

## *annie story*

Annie was a little girl who lived in a brown brick house with her mommy and daddy and a big black dog.[1]

Annie loved her mommy and daddy very much. Her daddy worked in a bank and went off to work every morning at 8:30 and came back home at 6:00. Annie was always the first to hear his car stop outside the house and then his footsteps coming up to the door. She would run to greet him, and Blackie, the dog, would run to greet him, too. Sometimes they would get all tangled up in each other. When Daddy opened the door, it looked like he was being greeted by a large, furry little girl.

Annie's mommy was a nurse. She worked at the hospital for only part of the day so that she could be home when Annie was home and at work when Annie was at school. She made Annie's breakfast each morning and took her to school, and then she came to pick her up at 3:00 when school was over.

When they got home, they would chat together while Mom did

---

[1]For this section, add your own details.

things around the house. Sometimes they went for walks, or Annie had friends over to play.

When Annie had friends over, they drank orange juice and ate toast with peanut butter and jelly. Annie liked to squish the peanut butter and jelly on all by herself. Then they played games. Sometimes they played dress-ups, or hide-and-seek. Sometimes they played tag with the dog.

Annie's friend usually left about 5:30. Then Annie would wait eagerly for her dad to come home so she could tell him everything that had happened to her that day.

Usually they all had dinner at 6:30. Annie used to like having dinner with her mom and dad, but lately she was liking it less and less. It seemed that her mom and dad just couldn't agree on anything. If her mom liked one thing, her dad didn't. If her dad liked something, her mom didn't. Sometimes it was nice all being together, but most often now her mom and dad argued or just sat silently around the table.[2] Annie didn't like it at all. She tried to tell them about all the good things she had done at school, hoping they would be proud of her and forget about disagreeing with each other. Sometimes she worried that they got cross at each other because of things she had done. Once, when she left her toys on the floor, her dad came home and yelled at her mom about the mess in the house. And her mom yelled back at him. Annie felt very bad that time.

What she hated most was when her mom and dad had arguments over her.[3] Sometimes Mom thought that Annie ought to be able to do one thing and Dad thought she shouldn't. Sometimes Dad complained that Mom spoiled her and Mom complained that Dad was too strict. They always started the same way, in low hard voices, as if they didn't want her to hear, and then their voices would get louder and louder and more and more angry. Annie wanted to run upstairs and hide under the bed and cover her ears so that she wouldn't have to listen.

---

[2]Again, add your own details. In some families, there are many loud fiery arguments before the divorce, in others it's all held in with prolonged silences.

[3]Children can feel like the meat in the sandwich in such situations. It adds to their sense of guilt over the divorce.

Sometimes, at night, she could hear them arguing.[4] At first she tried to pretend that it was the TV because she hated to hear them argue. When she couldn't pretend it was the TV anymore, she wriggled under the blankets, pressed her hands to her ears, and tried to think of something else so that she couldn't hear their voices.

She hated the sound of their voices when they were arguing. They sounded ugly and angry and hateful. It was hard to think of those voices as her loving mommy and daddy. She felt very sad and lonely as she lay in her room with the sound of those voices floating up the stairs and through the door.

When she woke in the morning, it was as if nothing had happened. Her mom gave her breakfast in her special cornflakes plate. Her dad smiled at her from behind his paper and said, "How's my darling daughter this morning?" Annie hoped that all the anger and fighting had gone away for good.

Usually, though, things were nice for a few days and then the arguments came back again. Annie hated them but she figured that all moms and dads must be like that. She had never had any other mom and dad, after all, so how could she know? Sometimes she looked at her friends' moms and dads, who seemed so happy together, and thought about them fighting in the downstairs room after dark.

Lately it seemed that Annie's mom and dad had been arguing more. Her mom seemed quieter than usual when she was with her, and her dad didn't seem to be home as much. He came home later and later from work, so that some days Annie hardly saw him at all.

Sometimes, when her mom was quiet and sad, Annie asked if something was wrong. Her mom would smile and say something like, "No, darling, it's just that I'm thinking about things."

Sometimes Annie worried that she had done something to make her mother sad and make her father stay away so much, but mostly she tried not to think about it and to pretend that it wasn't happening and would be better soon.[5]

---

[4]Parents who argue only at night when the children are in bed may imagine that their arguments and hostility go unnoticed. This is not often the case.

[5]Children may worry that it may be somehow their fault. It is important to reassure them on this point.

One day after dinner, Annie's mom said, "Your dad and I have to talk to you about something."[6] Annie felt a nasty, shivery feeling creeping all the way through her. She didn't know what it was, but she felt awful.

Her mom and dad sat down next to her and her mom began to speak.

"Darling," she said, "your dad and I have decided that we are unhappy living with each other and we've decided to get a divorce."

"That means we won't be married anymore," said her dad, "and we'll live in different houses."

Annie's mouth opened. She felt as if all her insides had suddenly dropped out through her feet. "But you can't," she said. "You can't get a divorce, you're my mommy and daddy." And she began to cry.

"Annie, darling," her mom said, and she looked as if she was almost crying, too, "we tried to stay together, but it makes us too unhappy."

"But why?" asked Annie. "Why can't you stay together?"

"Sweetheart," her father said, "when we met each other, long before you were born, we loved each other and that's why we got married. Then a lot of time went by and we started to change. We each started to like and dislike different things. We started not getting along with each other, and we were making each other miserable. We can't live together happily anymore, so it's best if we live separately and get a divorce."[7]

Annie's daddy went on, "A divorce means that we won't be married to each other anymore, but I'll still be your daddy and Mom will still be your mommy. That won't change."[8]

---

[6]It is best if both parents can break the news together. This prevents the information from being one-sided and allows the child to address questions to both parents. If there is more than one child in the family, it is generally preferable that they all be told at the same time. This allows the siblings to draw support from each other rather than having to keep the news secret. It also prevents one child breaking the news to a brother or sister before the parents have had a chance to do so themselves.

[7]Your explanations don't need to be complex. They can be as simple as this one.

[8]It's important to stress to your child that even though you are divorcing each other, you are not divorcing her. If, of course, one parent wants to have no further contact

"But if you loved each other before," said Annie, "why can't you just start loving each other again?"

"Love is very hard even for grown-ups to understand," said her mom. "We tried to keep loving each other, but it just didn't work."

"What will happen to me when you don't live together?" Annie asked.[9] She was suddenly very scared. What if they didn't want to live with her either? What if they wanted to divorce her?

"You'll stay here with Mommy, darling," said her dad. "I'm going to be moving out of the house soon."[10]

"But how will I see you?" asked Annie. She couldn't bear to think of not listening for her dad to come home again.

"You can come and visit me," said her dad, "whenever you like. You can come and stay on weekends."

"Why can't you stay here?" asked Annie. She didn't want to visit her dad. She wanted him to go on living with her.

"I can't stay here, Annie, because I won't be living here anymore," said her dad. "But you can come and stay with me. Mom and I will work out regular times for you to visit."[11]

"But I don't want to visit," Annie said, and began to cry again. Why couldn't her dad understand that she just wanted him to stay here and be with her? How could he love her if he wanted to live away from her?[12]

Her father shrugged his shoulders and looked at her mom. Her mom put her arms around Annie and said, "Come up to bed, darling, and we'll talk some more in the morning."

When Annie woke the next morning, she knew that something terrible had happened. Her body felt horrible and heavy, as if it didn't want to wake up, and she felt miserable inside. It took her brain a few minutes to remember exactly what it was that had happened.

---

with the child, a different explanation is necessary—see the introduction to this chapter for more details.

[9]This question is of dire importance to children. They may need continual reassurance on this subject.

[10]It is helpful to give children some notice of the divorce so that they have time to work things through.

[11]It is important for children to feel they can have good, consistent contact with the parent who is moving out.

[12]Children often find this hard to understand.

When she remembered, she rushed downstairs, terrified that Daddy had already left.

He was still there, though, looking a bit tired but eating his cornflakes as usual. For a moment Annie thought maybe it didn't really happen. Then Mom came in and Annie saw that she had been crying. She knew that it really had happened.

"Please don't go," she said to her daddy.

Daddy looked up very sadly. "I have to, Annie," he said.

Maybe, Annie thought, if she was very, very good, her parents would realize what a nice family they really had and not leave each other after all. That day, and the next, and the next, she did every single good thing she could think of doing. It was hard doing so many good things and being so very, very good all the time, but Annie thought that if she could just keep it up, her parents would stay together. But it didn't work.[13]

On Saturday, her dad moved to his new house. Annie felt so sad, she couldn't even speak. She went upstairs to her doll house and took the father doll out. "I'm going to punish you," she said. "Fathers are supposed to take care of their children." Then she took out the mother doll. "Mothers and fathers are supposed to stay together," she said. "You've been bad, bad, bad."[14]

That afternoon she felt very sick. Her tummy ached and her head ached and her eyes ached. She felt as if she were one big ache. "I think I'd better stay in bed this afternoon," she said to her mom. "Will you call Dad and tell him I'm very, very sick? If I'm sick, he has to come home to stay."[15]

Annie's mother gave her a kiss and smoothed her hair back. "Darling, Daddy still loves you, but he can't come back to stay—he's staying somewhere else now."

---

[13]This is a common reaction in children. Alternately, sometimes they can be very "bad" so as to bring the parents together in the common goal of controlling or helping them.

[14]Play helps children to work through some of the intense feelings that are aroused. It is common for anger to be among these.

[15]Sometimes children feel that if they are sick and helpless enough, the other parent will come back to look after them.

"Will you call him anyway?" asked Annie. She was sure that if her daddy knew how sick she was, he would come back to stay.

Later that afternoon, her father came upstairs. He gave her a kiss and said, "How are you, darling?"

Annie got so excited. "I knew you'd come back to stay," she told him.

"Annie, I haven't come back to stay," her daddy said. "Mommy and I aren't living together anymore. But I still love you and I'll always be your daddy and we'll still keep seeing each other."

"If you loved me, you wouldn't go away," said Annie.

"I know it's hard for you to understand," said her daddy, "but I promise I do still love you and I'll never stop loving you. You'll always be my daughter and I'll always be your daddy." He gave her a big hug.

But Annie shut her eyes and pretended not to hear or see. She didn't want a daddy who lived away from her. She wanted a daddy who lived here with her. She heard her daddy walk quietly down the stairs and she began to cry.

Sometimes when Annie thought about the divorce, she worried that it was something she had done that had made her dad want to leave home.[16] She remembered the times she had been naughty and her parents had had a fight over it. She wished she could take back that naughtiness and just have been a super-good girl all the time so her parents wouldn't have been able to fight over her. Maybe if they hadn't had so many fights, they wouldn't have gotten divorced.

Annie was scared to ask her mom about this because it made her feel so bad inside to think that maybe if she had been a better girl it wouldn't have happened. But one day, when they were going for a walk, her mom said to her, "You know, Annie, when parents get divorced, a lot of kids think it was their fault—that if they had been better kids, their parents wouldn't have separated."

"Really!" said Annie. She was very surprised to know that lots of kids felt like that.

---

[16]It is common for children to feel this. They need reassurance that the divorce is not their fault.

"I want you to know, darling," her mother went on, "that Daddy and I separating had nothing to do with you. You're a wonderful daughter and you always have been. We both love you very, very much and always will. Our divorce is because of the way we were with each other; it has nothing to do with you."

"Whose fault was it, Mommy?" asked Annie.[17] She had been thinking about this a lot. Sometimes she thought it was Daddy's fault because he had moved out of the house and left them; sometimes she thought it was Mommy's fault—that she had made Daddy so unhappy that he had to move out of the house. She kept thinking about it, but she hated thinking about it. When she got angry at Daddy because she thought it was his fault, she felt sad for Mommy and then sad for Daddy, too, because he was alone after all and she loved him. When she got angry at Mom and thought it was her fault, the same thing happened. She just didn't know whose side she was on. She wished she didn't have to take sides. It made her feel like she was split right in two and neither side was happy.

"It's no one's fault, darling," said Mommy. "No one's to blame. We both just changed and it wasn't right for us to stay married. Both of us are very sad that it ended this way. It's not like a football game where you have to cheer for one side and boo the other. And it's not like one of us did something very wrong to the other—it's not like TV where there are good guys and bad guys. We both said bad, angry things to each other when we were upset, but we did try to make it up. We just found that we couldn't get along and we would be happier apart."[18]

"What about me, though?" asked Annie. "If I ever said bad, angry things to you, would you divorce me?" She had been worry-

---

[17]Children are often told that one parent is to blame in a divorce, but apportioning blame to one or the other parent leaves children feeling split, disloyal, and distressed. You don't need to lie about being pleased with all your spouse's actions—they know you are not, that's why you divorced, after all—but try not to get them involved in taking sides.

[18]It's important to help children understand that divorce is not a simple black or white affair.

ing about this a lot. After all, if parents could divorce each other, why couldn't they divorce their kids?[19]

"We would never divorce you, Annie," said her mom. "It doesn't work that way for children. I will always be your mother and Daddy will always be your father. It doesn't matter how angry or mean we get with each other, I'll still be your mom and you'll still be my daughter. I'll always love you and look after you, and I'll never leave you. I'll always be here for you, darling."[20] And she gave Annie a great big kiss.

That weekend it was Dad's turn to have Annie. She went to stay at his new house every other weekend and he would call her during the week to say hi. Annie had his phone number, too, so that she could call him whenever she wanted.

At first she had hated coming to his home. Everything was new and strange to her, and it didn't seem right to be seeing her dad here when he really belonged at her house. But now she had gotten used to it.

Annie remembered the first time she had come to visit Dad in his new house. It had been really weird. It was her first weekend visit with him, and she had been looking forward to it for days. Her tummy felt like it was jumping up and down and she had trouble sitting still when she thought about it. She had woken early that morning and kept looking at her watch trying to make the hands go around faster so that Daddy would be here sooner. Suddenly there he was. Mommy was giving him Annie's little weekend bag to carry downstairs. It was really time to be going.

Annie had suddenly felt very scared. What if she didn't like it at Daddy's house? What if Daddy had changed and wasn't like he used to be? What if he couldn't take care of her properly? And then she saw Mommy preparing to wave good-bye. What if something happened to Mommy while she was away? What if Mommy wasn't

---

[19]It's important to reassure children on this point—that even if they are bad or angry, you won't "divorce" them.

[20]This explanation will have to be modified in the case where one parent is refusing to see the child. It is unreal and confusing to continue to tell the child that a parent who has disowned her still loves her and always will. It gives a very distorted idea of parental love.

there when she came back? What if Mommy was lonely while she was away?[21]

Annie's lower lip had begun to tremble and her eyes to feel hot, the way they did before she cried. She turned around to her mom.

"Annie," her mom had said, putting her arms around her. "It's really going to be all right. Daddy's new house might seem a bit strange at first, but he'll take good care of you. And I'll be fine here. When you come back tomorrow, I'll be waiting here for you." And she had given Annie a big hug.

The first few times that Annie had gone to visit at her dad's, he had seemed different from the way he used to be. For instance, he kept buying her things. All sorts of things. Almost anything she looked at, he would buy for her. At first it was fun, but then it got to feel sort of strange. It didn't feel normal. More than anything else, Annie wanted to feel normal. Also, her dad kept taking her out to things—to the zoo, to the circus, to the amusement park, to almost anywhere where there was noise and crowds and things to do. At first that was fun, too, but then Annie started to get tired of all the excitement and rides and sticky candy. When she got tired, she got grumpy. Often her dad got grumpy, too.[22]

One day she said to her dad, "Maybe we could just hang around the house today. We could play checkers, or I could help you wash your car."

"Sure," her dad said. He seemed happy. "Sure, we could do that. That would be just fine."

At her dad's new house, Annie had a special room that was hers. Her dad had asked her to come with him to pick out some of the things to put in it. Annie picked out some things she liked and it made her feel like the room really belonged to her.[23]

"What did you tell the kids at school about the divorce?" her dad

---

[21]The transition time between visits, that is, leaving or returning home, is often very anxiety arousing for children. They may need extra reassurance at this time. Let them know you'll be safe and waiting for them and that it is fine for them to have a good time with whichever parent they are visiting.

[22]This pattern is very common and not very helpful to children. See the introduction to this chapter for more discussion.

[23]It helps if the child has the sense that at least some part of the new house, even if it's only a corner, is specially hers.

asked one day.[24] They were drying dishes together, and he knew that Annie had been worried about how to tell her friends at school.[25]

"I just told them what you and Mom suggested," said Annie. "I said that my mom and dad were getting divorced and would be living in different houses. It wasn't as bad telling them as I thought it would be. Some of their parents are divorced, too, you know."

"Yes, I know," said her dad. "Divorce is very common and thousands of children have parents who are divorced."[26]

"Really?" asked Annie. She hadn't known there were that many. "My friend Betty's parents got divorced last year," she said. "Betty said her mom's always saying bad things about her dad and trying to get Betty to say them, too. She hates that."[27]

"Yes, it's terrible for children when their parents do that," said her dad.

"She said that every time she comes to one of their houses, the other spends hours and hours questioning her about every little thing they said and did. She says it makes her want to scream and not say a word for weeks."[28]

"That does sound horrible," said her dad. "Sometimes it's hard for parents because they get so angry with each other and feel so bad inside that they don't always do the right thing. You know what it's like when you get upset."[29]

"Yes," said Annie. She knew that when she got upset, she sometimes did really silly things.

---

[24]Children are often concerned about how to tell their friends. You might help them think of and practice appropriate phrases and explanations and work out how they will deal with questions.

[25]Experiencing access within a normal domestic situation is more helpful to the child that a constant swirl of amusement parks, presents, etc.

[26]It helps to let the child know that divorce is indeed common and that there are many, many children like her.

[27]This is very distressing for children. They feel pressured into taking sides and must cope with feelings of disloyalty, guilt, deceitfulness, etc.

[28]This is putting an enormous amount of pressure on children—they often feel like captured spies.

[29]It helps to explain to children that parents, too, are distressed and can behave irrationally.

"Will you and Mom ever get back together again?" asked Annie.[30]

"No," said her dad. "We'll always be your parents, but we'll never live together or be married again."[31]

Annie sort of knew that. At first after they had separated, she had kept hoping they would get back together. Her parents had always told her they wouldn't, but she had kept on hoping. Now she was kind of used to it, though, and somewhere inside her, she really knew that they would never live with each other again.

Annie's mother had to work more hours since the divorce because they needed the extra money. She took Annie to school in the morning, then went to work herself. She didn't get back until five o'clock. Mrs. Johnson from down the street picked Annie up from school and looked after her until her mother came home. Annie missed having her mom home after school. And her mom was tired after work and didn't have as much time to play as she used to.

Once, soon after Daddy had left, Annie had walked into the room to find Mommy just sitting and crying. Annie was frightened. It was scary to see a grown-up cry. Grown-ups were supposed to take care of you when you cried, not cry themselves.

"It's all right, Annie," her mom had said. "I know it's scary for you to see me cry. But all people have to cry sometimes when very sad things happen. Even grown-up people. I'll still be able to take care of you even when I'm sad. And after a while, the sadness will get better, too."

At first, when Annie's mom had started working more hours, Annie had been very miserable. It seemed like she hardly ever got to see her. She missed her dad and she missed her mom, too. She wished things could go back to the way they used to be.

At school she couldn't pay attention. She kept thinking about other things. When she tried to concentrate on her spelling, the

---

[30]Children take a long time to give up the hope that parents will get together. Sometimes even years after the final divorce, children are still entertaining this fantasy.

[31]It is important to be clear here and not build up unrealistic hopes which can only delay the healing process.

letters jumped out and jumbled themselves all over the page. She got 3 instead of her usual 9 for spelling that week. She felt very miserable.

"I've gotten stupid," she said to her mom. "I used to be able to do things at school and now I can't. I feel so dumb."[32]

"Honey," said her mom, giving her a big hug. "You're not stupid, you've been worried and miserable with all the things going on at home. When people get really worried, they can feel as if their brain's fogged up. They do silly things that they wouldn't usually do. They can't work properly or they trip over things and drop things. It happens to most people—it doesn't mean that they're stupid, just that they're worried or upset."

"Really?" said Annie. She felt relieved to think that she wasn't really dumb. And even more relieved to find that it happened to lots of people and not just her.

"Poor old Annie," said her mom, giving her another hug. "You've had a really rough time, haven't you. I haven't been able to be around as much as I used to, and I've probably been a bit grumpy when I have been around. I get more tired with all this extra work. You know what it's like when you're tired—it's much easier to get grumpy! Tell you what," she went on, "I've got a good idea—why don't we set aside a special time for just you and me each day. How about a half-hour before bedtime? We can play a game or tell a story or just chat. That way, no matter how busy I am during the evening, you'll always know that we'll have that time together."

"That sounds great!" said Annie. She felt better already. "That's a really good idea."[33]

Time went by and Annie started to feel better. There were still a lot of days when she wished Mom and Dad were back together again, but she was getting pretty used to the way things were now.

---

[32]Children may fail in all sorts of areas as a result of stress. Reassure them about their worth and ability and explain to them that many people react like this to stress. You might also want to go on to teach them relaxation as explained in Chapter 14.

[33]Finding some special time to be alone with your child in a loving, supportive way is one of the greatest gifts you can give her.

Her mom still worked hard, but they always had their time together before bed and that was nice. She stayed with her dad every other weekend. She liked being there now. Sometimes, after a whole weekend with Dad, she thought she saw even more of him than she did before the divorce. One day when her mom dropped her off at school, she said, "As a special treat today, I'm going to pick up your favorite chocolate cake on my way home from work."

"Oh, goodie!" said Annie. "Can Emily have dinner with us tonight?"

"Sure," said Annie's mom. "I'll call her mother and arrange it."

Annie could hardly wait for her friend Emily to come over, but when Emily came, instead of being her usual bouncy self, she looked very, very sad.

"My mom and dad are getting divorced," she said to Annie.

"When my mom and dad got divorced," Annie told her, "it was just awful."

"It's horrible, isn't it," said Emily.

"I felt so sad, I thought I was going to die," said Annie. "I didn't know I could feel so sad."

"What happens?" asked Emily. "What did you do?"

"I didn't really do anything," said Annie. "I just felt really sad. I talked with Mom and Dad a little. Then after a while I guess I started to get used to things. It just started to feel better. I still feel sad about it sometimes. But mostly I don't think about it much. I feel happy a lot of the time. Good things still happen, you know. You think they're going to stop happening—that nothing good will ever happen again. But they don't. Like after a bad dream, it sort of fades away and then you start to feel better again."[34]

"Oh." Emily looked doubtful. "Do you think that'll happen to me, too?"

Annie gave her hand a squeeze. "For sure it will," she said, and she took Emily's arm and led her out into the kitchen.

"Look," she said, "Mom's bought some cake specially for us."

The cake looked very fancy. It had shiny icing all over its top

---

[34]This is the positive ending, stressing that even though events may be painful and traumatic, one can still come through them to the light on the other side.

and around the sides. Right in the middle was a big, juicy straw-
berry with chocolate leaves. It stood out from the brown icing and
shone and glowed in the light like a little red heart.

"Here," said Annie, getting two plates. "A piece for me and a
piece for you."

# 10

# Stepfamilies

Stepfamilies are inevitably created out of a background of pain. A death or a divorce has led to this new family constellation. Given the complexities of adjustment to new relationships, even with the most benevolent of backgrounds, it seems foolish to imagine that creating a stepfamily will be simple or easy.

Creating a stepfamily is different from creating a marriage. In a marriage there are just two individuals to consider and both of you, presumably, are united in pursuit of at least one goal—that of becoming a happy, well-functioning couple. Creating a step family involves at least a third member and quite likely a number of extra members, none of whom may share your enthusiasm for, or vision of, the new family. They will also be at different stages of recovery from whatever traumatic experiences caused the original family to break up. They may have adjusted to, or become entrenched in, the new single-parent family that followed. They may or may not like you. They may like you but dislike what you stand for. They may have projected many of their fears, anxieties, and angers onto you—the outsider who makes the perfect scapegoat.

Equally, you may or may not like them. You may resent their demands and intrusions. You may experience them as a barrier to the intimacy and mutual supportiveness you saw as part of your new marriage. You may be unable to see the fear behind their hostility, the pain and insecurity behind their incessant demands. They are likely to have an equally incomplete view of you.

The prevailing myths of our society say that you are supposed to step into this turbulent brew and create instant bonds of love, friendship, and loyalty. All too many of us fall for the myths and become bitterly disappointed, guilt-ridden, and enraged when we discover that it just isn't so.

Of the several myths and misconceptions about stepfamilies, one of the most pervasive concerns the idea of instant love. There is a sense that on becoming a stepmother, for example, you must immediately love your stepchildren and, conversely, get them to love you. But just imagine for a moment that your husband, in a harem-minded mood and without your consent, has brought home a new wife to share your home with you. You wouldn't automatically love her even though she is a wonderful cook, does your washing and ironing for you each morning, and tries to be nice to you. Many stepchildren will see you in just such a role—the rival who is stealing their father's love and attention away from them.

Love, in general, doesn't happen instantaneously. It especially does not happen instantaneously in stepfamilies. Initially, at least, your stepchildren are likely to feel threatened by you and angry at you. You are seen as disrupting their security, taking their father away from them, wrecking their dream of reuniting their parents, trying to take the place of their natural mother, and so on. They may respond with overt or disguised hostility to your overtures. You may feel hurt or rejected. You may feel threatened by them. You may feel incompetent. You may feel humiliated by or angry at your inability to create the loving harmonious family of your fantasies. You may feel the children are eroding the relationship you have built up with your new spouse.

Instantaneous love under these conditions is an impossibility. Rather than setting out to love your stepchildren right away, it makes sense to give yourself short-term goals. The first is to get to know your stepchildren. Try to understand where they are coming from. Try to let them know that you recognize what they are feeling. Try to be fair-minded, friendly, and helpful toward them without casting yourself immediately as a loving mother. They know that love doesn't happen just like that. Rather than say "I love you" when you don't, you can say, "Love takes time to grow. I want to get to love you."

It's disconcerting when stepchildren return our friendliest efforts with hostility. They must be nasty, malicious kids, we tell ourselves. We don't feel like the enemy, so why should we be treated as the enemy? We forget that their perceptions are different from ours. They have good reason, after all, to see us as the enemy—we are breaking up their relationship with their father, intruding into their territory, perhaps bossing them around, all without even a by-your-leave. We chose this situation—they did not. And although their attacks may seem personal, it is worth remembering that anyone who stepped into your position would be treated in exactly the same fashion.

It is important to expect that there will be initial difficulties and to give yourself time to deal with and resolve these. "Time" in terms of a stepfamily usually means years. Some experts believe that it takes from three to seven years to become a stable family unit. Starting off with high expectations and a short timetable is courting disaster.

Another misconception is that a stepfamily will function like a biological family. It won't because it isn't. For the children, a biological family has a long and shared history. Love has been able to grow over a lifetime. The roles of the different members have been shaped and solidified over many years.

In contrast, members of a stepfamily have had their roles fractured, changed, and even severed. The only child may now be forced to share the nest with stepsiblings. The oldest girl may now find she is outranked by two older stepsisters. You, the stepparent, are a relative stranger. The parent who gave the children all his attention is now sharing it with you. And to make it worse, all this is on top of whatever trauma led to the family being broken up in the first place.

When there are two sets of children, it is clear that they have differing relationships with the parent and stepparent. One set of children will have close emotional ties with their biological parent, the other set of children will lack these ties to that parent.

The rules that apply to biological families need to be changed for stepfamilies.

Don't expect to step into a family and love your own and your stepchildren equally—that would be living a lie. It is natural that your bonds with your own children are deeper than those with stepchildren. There is no need to feel guilty about this. Your new spouse, too, is likely to have similar feelings toward his children and stepchildren. Accept it and recognize that with time, the bonds with stepchildren will hopefully deepen and stabilize. In the meantime, make an effort to treat all the children fairly.

Don't try to take the place of the children's natural parent. Don't get into a competition over who is the "better" parent, and don't try to split the children's loyalties. Let your stepchild know that you do not want to take away from her relationship with her natural mother and that you know you cannot replace her. You are different people and you play different roles in the child's life. Children often feel they are being disloyal to their natural mother if they like you. It can be helpful to let them know that you understand their feelings, but that liking two people does not mean that you are being disloyal to one of them.

Give children time to be alone with their natural parent, your spouse. This time is as essential to your well-being as it is to theirs. The more left out they feel, the more stressful family life is likely to become. Try, too, to find some time for just you and your spouse to be alone.

Make your marital relationship a focus of primary importance. Do not allow yourselves to be split as a couple over parenting issues. Try to understand, support, and discuss one another's viewpoints. If you want his support in changing his child's behavior, don't start by attacking his child—"She's selfish, spoiled, vicious," etc. This will make him spring to his child's defense. If someone attacked your child like this, you would probably have the same defensive reaction. Instead, focus on how difficult and painful you find his child's interactions and ask whether he could help.

Do not rush straight into being a disciplinarian. If you wish to take on this role, do it slowly. A natural parent's discipline is backed up by a relationship stretching back for years. Children are likely to revolt if a newcomer suddenly starts laying down the law.

Many men moving into the stepfather role find that it has its own difficulties. Sometimes men expect, or are expected by their wives, to be the new disciplinarian of the family. But it can be difficult to become the disciplinarian father without any of the background and preparation needed for the role—that is, a lifetime's knowledge of the child and a relationship based on respect and trust. Knowledge, respect, and trust all take time to build up and, without them, disciplining is a much harder job.

Different families find different solutions work best for them. For many families, initially at least, things work better when each parent disciplines his or her own children. For others, it's more comfortable when one parent disciplines both sets of children. Sometimes an attempt by a stepfather to discipline a child is seen as an attack on that child's relationship with her natural father— "Only my real dad can tell me what to do!" Sometimes if a stepfather holds back on disciplining, it is interpreted by the child as "He doesn't care about me."

Working out your new roles and how they fit in your particular family constellation requires patience, time, and the ability to be flexible in finding out what works best for you.

In all that you do, go slowly and proceed with caution. Keep your expectations low and long-term rather than high and short-term.

Try to find support or counseling if it all feels too much for you. There are support groups for stepparents. You may want to see a marriage or family counselor for help as a couple or as a family. There is also the option of individual counseling to help you sort things out.

## *annie story*

Annie was a little girl who lived in a brown brick house with her mommy and her dog called Blackie.[1]

Her daddy used to live there with them, too, but two years ago Annie's mom and dad got a divorce and her daddy went to live in another house. Annie was seven when that happened, and it was the worst year of her life. She missed her dad and she was

---

[1]Change the details to suit your child.

angry at him for leaving her. Sometimes she was angry at her mom for not being able to make him stay. Sometimes she was angry at herself. For that whole year Annie was sad all the time, and almost all the time she was worried.[2] She worried about all sorts of things. She worried about whether her father was lonely; she worried about whether her mother would always be sad; she worried about what her friends would think; she worried about whose fault the divorce was; she worried about what would happen to her; she worried about whether her mom or dad would divorce her; she worried about what she'd done and what she would do. She worried and worried.[3]

One of the horrible things about divorce, she thought, was that it made everything change. All the things that Annie was used to—her dad coming home at night, the walks she used to take with him and Blackie, the way he used to butter her toast in the morning—all those things changed. And she couldn't do anything about it. And then, just when she thought she had got used to the changes, things changed some more.[4]

Mommy met Josh. At first, Annie didn't take much notice of Josh, and Mommy didn't talk about him much. Then Mommy started to talk about him more, and he started to be there more. Soon, every time Annie looked up, Josh was there, having meals with them, going on outings with them, watching TV with them. It seemed like there wasn't any time anymore when Annie had Mommy to herself. She began to hate Josh.[5] Annie didn't seem to count when Josh was around. Mommy sometimes didn't pay any attention to Annie—she was busy with Josh. Annie worried that Josh was going to take up more and more of Mommy's time

---

[2] Children are often awash with intense, confusing, and painful emotions in the wake of a divorce.

[3] Children often worry a great deal about their parent's welfare after a divorce. Parents may foster this by trying to gain the "sympathy vote" from their children. This places a great deal of extra stress on the child and should be avoided.

[4] Divorce is a process, not a single, static event. There are many different phases of this process, all of which require adjustment, too. Just when you've adjusted to one phase, you need to adjust to another.

[5] Children often see their parent's new relationship as a direct threat. They fear that there will be less time and love available for them.

and there would be even less for her. Maybe there might even be none at all. Maybe now that Mommy had Josh, she might not want Annie. Annie hated Josh even more.

One day, Mommy told Annie that she and Josh were going to get married. Annie was so upset, she couldn't even speak. She rushed upstairs to her room and fell on the bed and cried. If Mommy married Josh, that meant that Mommy couldn't marry Daddy again![6] Annie didn't even want to think about that! She didn't want to live with horrible old Josh. She already had a father, and it wasn't Josh! No way was Josh going to take her daddy's place.[7]

After Josh and Mom got married, Annie got more and more unhappy and more and more bad tempered. Her mother tried to talk to her, but she didn't want to listen. Josh tried to talk to her and sometimes even bought her little presents, but Annie wasn't going to be nice to him. If she couldn't have her dad back, at least she could have her mom all to herself. There wasn't any place for Josh in this house. She wished she could make him see that.

One night Annie lay in bed feeling miserable as usual. "If only Josh would disappear," she thought. "Things would be so much better. If only Mom and Dad were married again. I'm sure I would be happy . . . If only . . ." But she had drifted off to sleep.

She woke to hear the chiming of the big town hall clock. "One," it chimed, "two, three, four, five, six, seven, eight, nine, ten, eleven, twelve, thirteen."

"Thirteen?" thought Annie. No, she must have counted wrong. She was just turning over to go to sleep again when there was a mighty bump and then a crash and then the sound of someone hopping around on one foot saying, "Ooh, ooh, ooh . . ."

Annie sat up in bed and stared. The "ooh's" were coming from the strangest lady she had ever seen. Half her hair was white and pulled back into the primmest, most proper bun that any grandma

---

[6]Children often cling to the fantasy that Mommy and Daddy will remarry for much longer than most parents generally realize.
[7]Children often feel very angry at the thought that a stepparent is trying to take a parent's place. They may feel that being nice to the stepparent is being disloyal to the noncustodial parent.

ever wore. But the other half was tomato ketchup red and flew about her face in frizzy curls that looked as if they had been styled by a tornado. She wore half a pair of eyeglasses that miraculously balanced on her nose. Her thick fleecy coat was piled on top of a light, summery dress. And the foot on which she was hopping wore a heavy brown hiking boot, while the other foot wore a thin, high-heeled dancing sandal.

"I can see why she lost her balance," thought Annie, and then she gave a sudden "Oh!" For she had just looked up and seen that out of the back of the lady's brown, curly coat, which looked like a bear and a sheep had gotten tangled up in it, sprouted a pair of delicate, silver wings. "Oh, my goodness," thought Annie, sitting up even straighter. This was not the sort of person you expected to meet in your room. Even at thirteen o'clock at night.

The lady gave a final hop and landed near Annie's bed.

"Do you mind if I sit down?" she asked, settling herself down before Annie could answer. But even the way she sat on the bed was strange. First she sat in one position and then in another. She tucked her leg up under her and then, changing her mind, untucked it and gave it a good shake. She folded her arms and then unfolded them. She leaned back on her elbows, then she sat up straight.

Finally, Annie said timidly, "Please, do you think you could settle in one position? You're making me dizzy."

"Oh," said the lady, looking as if Annie had made the most impossible request. "Oh, very well. I'll try." And she did. But not without tremendous effort. You could see her arms and legs twitching occasionally as they attempted to change positions.

"Who are you?" asked Annie. Now that the lady was sitting still, Annie could see that she had a very nice twinkly face and bright blue eyes, even if they did look a bit strange with only half a pair of glasses.

"My dear, you wished for me," said the lady. "I came almost as soon as I heard you. I would have come sooner," she added apologetically, "but I couldn't decide whether I should put a coat on or not."

"Oh," said Annie. She tried to remember what she had been wishing for, and how long ago.

"I'm the If-only Fairy," said the lady, in a helpful tone. "I'm in charge of all the 'if only' wishes made in this world. And believe me, there are a lot of them," she added darkly.

"Oh," said Annie, suddenly remembering what she had been thinking before she went to sleep. "You mean you make 'if only' wishes come true?"

"I'm here to let you see what it would be like if they did," said the lady, smiling and nodding and attempting to untangle one red curl that had got caught in her eyelashes.

"Why is your hair like that?" asked Annie, and then bit her lip, because put like that it sounded kind of rude.

But the If-only Fairy didn't seem to mind. "Well, I love the color red," she said, patting the red side fondly, "and I always wanted curly hair, but sometimes I think, 'If only it was smooth and white and tied back, I'd look so much more wise and elegant.' It's like shoes," she said, holding out her feet to examine them. "I love these high-heeled fancy sandals, but when you get a blister, you think, 'if only I'd worn comfy walking shoes.' So I do. Everything all at once. That way I don't have to make choices." She turned to Annie. "Good solution, don't you think?"

Annie looked polite. Privately she thought it wasn't a good solution at all. Apart from looking silly, you'd never even get to walk properly.

"Well, let's get down to your if-onlys," said the lady, settling herself more comfortably on the bed.

"You mean I can get all my if-onlys to come true?" asked Annie.

"I'll show you how," said the lady, flicking her fingers and producing an enormous drawing pad and six colored pencils out of thin air.

"Golly," said Annie. "How did you do that?"

"Easy," said the Fairy, but she was already gazing at the drawing pad and muttering, "Is that the best size, I wonder? Maybe I should have a bigger size. If only . . ."

"No, no," said Annie, who wanted to get on with things. "That's a fine size, that's just right." She didn't want the If-only Fairy to spend the next hour flicking different sized drawing pads out of the air and not getting anything done.

"Oh, all right," said the Fairy. She looked a bit disappointed. "Are you sure it's the size you want?"

"Yes, yes," said Annie. "Now please, tell me what I do."

"Well," said the Fairy, "all you have to do is draw your if-only on this magic pad, breathe on it three times, and watch what happens."

"You mean I can draw any if-only at all?" asked Annie, for she had suddenly had a great idea—she was going to turn Josh into a toad!

"Yes," said the Fairy, "anything at all."

So Annie took the pencils and drew. First she drew a big ugly toad and put a little collar on it marked with a J so that it would know that it was Josh. Then she drew her mother jumping away from the toad, and finally she drew herself with a big smile on her face.

"Now what do I do?" she asked the Fairy.

"Breathe on it three times," said the Fairy, "and each time you say to yourself, 'Come true, come true—I command you to.'"

"All right," said Annie, and, feeling very excited, she did just that.

Something very strange happened. As soon as her last breath had touched the paper, the figures Annie had drawn began to move. There was a popping sound and Annie let out a little shriek for she suddenly felt herself being pulled forward. She put out her hands to break her fall, but instead of the wall she found herself touching something large and cold and slimy—a TOAD!

"Eeek!" yelled Annie. She didn't like toads, and most of all she didn't like muddy, slimy toads who had just crawled out of a pond. The toad looked at her with a funny expression on its face as if it was trying to say something but had forgotten the words. Experimentally it hopped closer and landed on Annie's foot.

"Help!" shrieked Annie. "Oh, Yuck! Help!" Suddenly there was another popping sound and she found herself sitting back in bed. The If-only Fairy stared at her with a rather worried expression.

"Well, by the sounds of it, that one didn't work out the way you wanted it to," she said.

"No," said Annie. "It didn't work out at all." She thought for a minute. "Can I try another one?" she asked. She had just had a good idea. This time she would just make Josh disappear.

Busily she drew a room in her house. In it she drew herself. Next to her she drew her mother with a smile on her face. No Josh was in sight. In fact, there was no Josh anywhere at all.

"Do I do the same thing again now?" she asked the IOF, for that was what she had decided to call her. To herself, at least.

"Yes," said the IOF, with what seemed to be a very knowing look in her eyes.

This time Annie was prepared for the pop and the rush forward. What she was not prepared for was the expression on her mother's face as she stood next to her. The smile that Annie had drawn had turned to a look of tired sadness.

"What's wrong?" asked Annie, feeling awful to see her mother looking like that.

"Nothing, darling," said her mother. "It's just that sometimes I get lonely and feel a bit sad."

"Why don't you ring up Josh?" said Annie, and then bit her lip. Why on earth was she saying that?

"Josh?" said her mother, looking puzzled. "Who's Josh?" She sat down by the TV set and gazed through it into the distance.

"Help!" called Annie to the IOF. "You'd better get me out of this one, too!"

"Having a bit of trouble, my dear?" asked the Fairy when Annie had returned. "These things can be a shade more difficult than one expects, you know."

"They certainly can," said Annie, feeling worried—there just had to be a way.

"I know!" she said triumphantly. "I know just what to do now!" She had suddenly remembered that she could draw her mother and father back together again. Working carefully, with her tongue poked slightly out between her teeth to help her concentration, she drew her mother and father smiling up at each other and holding hands. Next to them she drew herself, also smiling. Then she breathed three times on the picture and waited. "Pop!" She was pushed into the picture. The first thing she noticed was that her mother had let go of her father's hand.

"How can you say that!" her mother was saying to her father. The smile had gone from her face.

"If you were just a bit more organized, I wouldn't have to come home to this mess!" said her father, his voice growing louder with every word. He, too, had stopped smiling.

"If you'd lift just one finger to help me, there wouldn't be such a mess," said Annie's mother, her face looking grim and angry.

"Lift a finger!" said her father. "I slave away at the office all day and you want me to come home and slave some more!"

"Well what about me?" shouted her mother, nearly in tears. "I work too! Why does everything have to be my responsibility?"

Annie cringed. She had forgotten what it was like when her mom and dad had lived together. Sadly she called out for the IOF.

"It's not fair," she said to the Fairy. "Even though you say I can make my if-onlys happen, I can't make anything change."

"Ah," said the Fairy. "That's because you've been going about it the wrong way."

"What do you mean?" asked Annie.

"You've been trying to change things by making other people change. That's difficult to do, you know. Other people have minds of their own. Just wishing they'd change usually isn't enough to make a difference."

"Well, what does then?" Annie's voice trembled. "What does make a difference? How can I make things change?" She was very upset. She had really wanted to change things, and now it didn't seem to be possible.

"I'll show you," said the IOF kindly. She patted Annie's shoulder. "I know you're upset, but there is a way to make things different." She handed the colored pencils to Annie. "Now," she said, "draw me a picture of your family just as the people in it usually are."

Annie thought for a few minutes. Then she drew her mother and Josh sitting at the dinner table. They were smiling and talking. Annie drew herself at the other side of her mother, facing Josh. She put a big scowl on her face. She looked very mean and bad-tempered. Just the way she usually looked around Josh.

"Now," said the IOF, "remember what you did in the first

picture—you drew Josh differently and tried to change him. That didn't work, did it?"

"No," said Annie. "It sure didn't."

"Then," said the IOF, "in the third picture you tried to change your mother by drawing her differently—with your father."

"And that didn't work either," said Annie.

"Right," said the IOF. "Now, in this picture you can change someone who will make a difference."

"Who?" asked Annie. There didn't seem to be anyone left to change.

"Yourself, of course," said the Fairy. "Changing the way you are yourself can make a *big* difference."[8]

"Oh," said Annie. She hadn't thought of that. She paused.

"How do I do it?" she asked. She was a bit puzzled, but it sounded promising.

"Just do another drawing," the IOF said, "and this time, instead of that frown on your face, draw a pleasant expression."

"Okay," said Annie, and she did. She breathed on it three times and then, Pop!, she was in the picture.

The first thing she noticed was how nice it felt. She had a smile on her face and was in a good mood.

"Would you like some more potatoes, Annie?" Josh asked.

"Yes," said Annie. The potatoes had been delicious. Then she remembered to say "Thank you" and smiled at Josh.

Josh looked startled, then he smiled back. For the first time, Annie noticed that Josh had a very nice smile. She looked over at her mother. She was smiling, too. She seemed proud of Annie, pleased that she was being nice to Josh.

"Can I go over to Emma's after lunch?" asked Annie. "I can ride my bike over."

"Sure," said her mother.

"Oh," said Annie—she had just remembered that her bike had

---

[8]Children often feel particularly helpless during the process of divorce and remarriage. Major changes are occurring that profoundly affect their lives and yet there seems to be nothing they can do about them. This story reminds them that they do, in fact, have the ability to influence the quality of their lives.

a flat tire. "I won't be able to go, because my front tire has a
puncture."

"I'll patch it for you," said Josh.

"Oh, thanks!" said Annie. "That would be great!"

Josh looked pleased.

Annie smiled at him again. It felt a bit strange. She wasn't used
to smiling at Josh. But it didn't feel bad. Actually, it felt quite good.

Annie looked at Josh. He was smiling at her. Maybe he wasn't
really all that bad. After all, she thought, it *was* very nice of him
to patch her tire for her.

Josh went off to get his tools, and Annie's mom came up to her
and gave her a hug.

"Annie," she said. "I'm so pleased that you're being nice to Josh.
It makes me really happy."

Annie smiled.

"It means a lot to Josh, too," her mom went on. "He thought
you hated him, and he felt terrible."

"Oh," said Annie. She didn't know what to say.

"You know," her mom said, "I've been wanting to talk to you
about this, but you were so bad-tempered up till now that it was
hard to talk to you properly. I know you've been upset about Josh
and me getting married. I thought that you might be worried that
now you'd have to make Josh your dad instead of your daddy."

"I was," said Annie sadly.

"But, darling, Josh knows that he won't ever take the place of
your dad and he doesn't expect to. He's someone different from
your dad. But he'd still like to help take care of you."[9]

"Oh," said Annie. She felt a bit better to hear that. "You know,"
she said, "when you and Josh got married, I felt really bad because
then you couldn't marry Dad again." As soon as she had said that,
she felt a bit silly. But that was what she had been thinking.

"Oh, Annie," said her mom, giving her another hug. "I didn't
realize you were still thinking that your dad and I might get
together again. There has never been any chance of that happen-

_____

[9] It is helpful to make clear to children that the stepparent is not trying to take the
place of their parent.

ing, even without Josh. We were married once, but we never ever will be again. That part of our lives is past." And she gave Annie another hug.

"Oh," said Annie, feeling sad again. Deep down, she thought, she had really known all along that her mom and dad wouldn't get back together.

"And you know, darling," her mom went on, "I want you to know that just because Josh is here, that doesn't mean I love you any less.[10] You're my very special, very own daughter and I will always, always love you. But you know, just like you like having friends your own age to play with and be best friends with, so do grown-ups need people their own age. Liking Emma so much and spending all that time with her doesn't stop you from loving me, and my feelings for Josh don't stop me from loving you."

"Oh," said Annie again, feeling much better. It felt good to hear Mommy say that.

Mommy cuddled Annie tight. "I think it's terrific the way you've started being nice to Josh. He really wanted you to like him, you know. But he just doesn't know what to do. It's wonderful the way you're showing him how to be friends with you."[11]

"I'm . . .?" said Annie, astonished. But she never had the chance to finish the sentence because there was a loud pop and she was back in her bed.

"Golly," said Annie. "That was certainly different!" She turned to the IOF. "You mean it was me that made all those changes happen?"

"It sure was," said the Fairy. "After all, you and I wouldn't be having nearly so much fun together if you'd been snapping and snarling at me all the time." She gave a frown. "I can get pretty mean when people snap and snarl at me. I don't like it one little bit."

"I never thought of it that way," said Annie. "I guess I wasn't giving Josh much of a chance to be nice, was I?"

"I guess you weren't," said the Fairy. "But it's not too late to try

---

[10]Reassuring children that they're not going to "lose" you is important. They often harbor fears that they will be less important to you or that you will love them less now that you have a new spouse.

[11]This puts Annie in a position of strength. Instead of feeling like a maligned and resentful victim, she can see herself as a helpful teacher.

it out. Sometimes, of course, it takes people a while to be really sure that things are different. Sometimes it takes them a while to react. So you may need to be patient."

"You know, I think I'd like to try it," said Annie. "It did feel a lot more fun than the way things have been lately." She turned to the IOF. "You really think I could make things change the way I did in the picture?"

"I really think you can," said the Fairy. And she gave Annie a comforting pat on the shoulder. "But right now I think you'd better get some sleep." She tucked Annie back into the bed. "Sweet dreams," she said, "and remember, I'll be watching over you. I know you're going to be a success!" Then with a bump and a few wiggles she flew out of the room.

The next morning Annie woke up with a good feeling. She thought about the adventure she had had last night with the If-only Fairy. She remembered the IOF saying that she, Annie, had the power to change things. She felt very important when she thought about that.[12] She decided that she was going to begin changing things that very morning.

She started by smiling at Josh at breakfast. Josh looked startled but pleased, just like he had last night.

He smiled back at Annie. "It's good to see you looking happy," he said.

"I guess I have been pretty grumpy lately," said Annie.

Josh paused. "I guess it's been hard for both of us," he said.

Annie looked at him, surprised. "How do you mean?" she asked. "How has it been hard for you?"

"Well, you know how you've never had a stepdad before? I've never *been* a stepdad before, so it's all new to me. I'm still learning."

"Oh," said Annie. She paused. "I never thought of it like that," she said. "You mean it's been weird for you being a stepdad just like it's been weird for me having a stepdad?"[13]

---

[12]Children's self-esteem is often low during the process of divorce and remarriage. When their self-esteem is raised, they are often more able to interact in a positive way.
[13]It can come as a surprise for children when they see things from the stepparent's

"Well," said Josh, "parts of it have been nice, but parts of it have been weird."

"Like what?" asked Annie.

"Well, for instance," said Josh, "I know I'm not your dad because you have a dad. I would never try to take the place of your dad because you already have one."

Annie nodded. She was surprised to hear Josh say that. "When you married Mom, I thought you were trying to take Dad's place," she said. "It made me feel really mad at you."

"I don't want to do that," said Josh, "but I do want to be the best stepfather that I can be for you."

"Well, if a stepfather's not the same as a father, what exactly is it that a stepfather does?" Annie asked. "How do you get to be a good stepfather?"

"That's exactly what I've been trying to work out," said Josh. "The way I figure it, part of being a stepfather is being a friend, but there's more to it than that."

"How do you mean?" asked Annie.

"Well, as well as being a grown-up friend, now that I'm married to your mom and living in the house with you, I also have a responsibility to help her take care of you. Taking care of kids means all sorts of things. Some of it means doing fun things with kids. Some of it means helping kids learn things. Some of it means disciplining kids when they do something wrong."

"I hate it when you tell me what to do and try to boss me around," said Annie. "You're not my father and you shouldn't tell me what to do."

"I know it feels very different when your father disciplines you than when I do," said Josh. "You see, you've had lots of years to love your dad in and to know that he loves you. When someone you love and who loves you tells you to do something, it's a nicer feeling than when someone you barely know does. Especially when you're mad at that someone and you think he doesn't like you anyway."

---

point of view. They have often built up such a hostile picture in their mind that the step parent comes out as Super-Villain with no saving graces whatsoever.

"Like you, you mean," said Annie, thoughtfully.

"Yes," said Josh. "Except that you're wrong about me, I do like you. There are lots of great things about you. I keep wishing we could get along better and enjoy the good things about each other."

"But you don't love me like my mom and dad do," said Annie.

"No one loves anyone in exactly the same way," said Josh. "You love your mom and dad, but you don't love each of them in exactly the same way."

"That's true," said Annie.

"Also," said Josh, "we haven't had much of a chance to really get to know one another. You can't love someone if you don't really know them. Getting to love people takes time because getting to know people takes time. But I know that I would like to get to love you. And I'm sure that if we give each other a chance and get to know each other properly, that will happen."

Annie nodded slowly. "I hadn't thought about it like that," she said. She thought for a moment. "That would be nice. That would mean that I had three people loving me instead of just two."

"That's right," said Josh.

"That sounds good," said Annie.

"You know," said Josh, "this must have been a really tough time for you. Some kids feel like they're being churned around in a washing machine. They have so many feelings and the feelings are all mixed up with each other."

Annie nodded. "That's just what it feels like," she said. "One of the really bad things is when I go from one house to the other. You know, when I go to stay with Daddy for a couple of days and then I come back here."

Josh nodded. "That must be hard for you," he said.

"Yes," said Annie, "it is. And also when I'm at Dad's, I get used to the way he does things. Then when I come back here, you do things differently. You and Mom have different rules than he does."

"That must get pretty confusing for you," said Josh.[14]

---

[14]Children can find the transition between households, with their different sets of

Annie nodded.

"I wish it didn't have to be so hard for you," said Josh. "I wonder if there's any way we can make it easier." He thought for a few minutes.

"I have a good idea," he said. "What if you and your mom and I all got together and wrote down our family rules? Then we could make them into a song—you could pick your favorite tune and we could make the rules into funny rhymes."

Annie laughed.

"Then," said Josh, "whenever you come home after being at your dad's, we could all get together and sing the family song. That might make it easier and a bit more fun for you."

"I like that idea," said Annie. "I bet I could make up some really funny rhymes."[15]

Josh smiled. "How about we make a fresh start?" he said, and he held out his hand. "It'll take time and we'll have to go slowly, but I think we can work things out. We'll be patient with each other, and we'll try to talk to each other about what we're feeling. I'm sure I'll still do some things that you don't like and you'll do some things that I don't like, but that happens in families even when there aren't any stepparents. When it happens, we can get together and figure out what to do about it."

Annie smiled. She held out her hand and shook Josh's hand. "Okay," she said. "It's a deal."

---

rules and expectations, very difficult. Added to this is the fact that leaving one household for the next also means leaving, albeit temporarily, a parent.

[15] A touch of humor can often defuse difficult situations.

# 11

# Impulsive Children

The impulsive child is a little like the quiz contestant who presses the buzzer before he's had time to think of the answer. The quiz contestant simply loses points in a contest. The impulsive child loses more than that. Her behavior can cause frustration, anger, and unhappiness, not just within herself but in the people around her.

Impulsive children react without thinking, often in inappropriate and sometimes in destructive ways. They haven't learned how to plan ahead, to consider alternatives or consequences, or to delay the immediate gratification of their desires.

Impulsive behavior is generally present in hyperactive children, but it is possible to be impulsive without being hyperactive. Other qualities that often go hand in hand with impulsivity are a short attention span and a high level of distractibility.

Younger children are more impulsive than older children. Maturity brings an increasing ability to pause, evaluate, and plan before leaping into action. Some studies suggest that the incidence of extreme impulsivity is similar to that of hyperactivity, that is, 5 to 10 percent of all children. Another 10 percent are considered impulsive enough to cause fairly regular problems for themselves and the people around them.

Extreme impulsivity may have an organic basis, ranging from neurological dysfunction to genetic predisposition. For some children, impulsivity may be a learned behavior. They may have modeled themselves on impulsive members of the family, for instance, or been rewarded for being quick rather than thoughtful or painstaking. They may never have been taught how to substitute long-term gratification for short-term gratification.

Anxious, panicky, or depressed children are less able to think clearly or plan ahead. They are therefore more prone to acting on impulse in an unconsidered and often destructive way.

Researchers have shown that overly impulsive children can be helped to change their behaviors. Through the medium of "self-talk," they can be taught to stop, reflect, and plan before reacting.

Self-talk is our inner conversation with ourselves. We all do it. Even those who think they don't talk to themselves have probably spent the last few seconds saying to themselves, "Do I talk to myself? No, I don't talk to myself," before deciding that they don't talk to themselves!

Impulsive children need to be taught how to use self-talk as a buffer between impulse and too-hasty action. When faced with a problem, the child is taught to talk herself through five steps that involve defining the problem, picking the best approach to it, focusing attention on it, choosing an answer, and praising herself for a job well done.

This approach works best if it is first demonstrated, or modeled, by the parent, therapist, or teacher. The adult begins by talking herself through the problem out loud. Next, the child is encouraged to write down the five steps on a card, using the child's own phraseology. The child then talks herself through a problem. After the child has had some practice at this, the adult tones her voice down to a whisper as she talks herself through a problem. The child is encouraged to follow suit. Finally, the adult uses silent self-talk, with appropriate nonverbal actions, such as stroking the chin, etc., to indicate that thinking processes are going on.

When teaching these methods, go slowly and take them a step at a time. The child should read the five steps from her card until they become so familiar that they are committed to memory.

There are two kinds of models the adult can act out while teaching the child how to self-talk. One is the "mastery" model in which everything goes smoothly and no mistakes are made. The second is the "coping" model in which the adult deliberately makes a slip-up in order to show the child how to cope with a mistake. Children are more likely to imitate a coping model, and it gives them more flexibility in real-life problem solving where trial and error can be a part of the process. In modeling how to cope with errors and failures, the emphasis is on keeping them in perspective. For example, the appropriate self-talk would be, "I made a mistake. Never mind, I'll do better next time," rather than, "I made a mistake, I'm hopeless. I'll never get this right."

Problem-solving techniques using self-talk can also be applied to social situations. Aggressive behavior often results when an impulsive child who is being teased or who feels frustrated lashes out without thought.

Using the same technique as before, children are taught to talk themselves through these situations. The following steps are used: The child identifies the problem, including the emotions it has aroused in her. She then thinks of several alternative ways of responding. She looks at the likely consequences of each alternative and then decides which course of action to pursue. The story following gives an example of this process.

In working with your child, it is helpful to work through a number of different situations so that the child can practice applying these techniques to a variety of problems. Some examples are: Your friend doesn't want to play the same game as you do; you and your sister both want the last banana left on the fruit plate; and so on.

Because impulsive children find it hard to delay short-term gratification, it is helpful to teach them methods of handling this problem. You can teach them to use self-talk, for example, "I have to wait for fifteen minutes before it's my turn to play with the video game. I'll play with my sticker collection while I wait, and that will make the time go faster."

You can also teach them to use their imagination to help stave off the frustration of waiting. For example, if a promised new baseball glove is not going to materialize until tomorrow, you could show your child how to play an exciting game of baseball and polish her skill as a catcher, all in her imagination. You might want to use the Annie Story on relaxation (Chapter 14) as a guide and simply substitute baseball-oriented activities for magic carpets and the like. Or you can start straight in with a question that engages the child, such as "If you were playing baseball, who would you pick to be part of your team?" and then guide your child into the game as it begins. The child can usually take over quite readily at that point. Most children have a wonderfully vivid capacity for this sort of fantasy fun.

It is worth remembering, too, that when asking an impulsive child to do a task, the more concrete and specific you can be, the easier it will be for her to pick it up. For instance, instead of saying, "I'd like you to put your dirty clothes in the wash basket," it helps to demonstrate the task: walk your child through the actions involved so the job is broken down into in manageable bits as opposed to an amorphous and possibly overwhelming whole. Set the task out in simple steps.

Impulsive children are usually easily distracted, but there are ways of overcoming this tendency. A good first step is to make sure that the desk or table at which they do homework is uncluttered and as free of distractions as possible.

You can also play a game with your child by getting her to complete a set piece of work while you do distracting things around her, like sweeping the floor near her feet. If your child completes her task, she gets a star or some other reward. Keep the distractions minimal and the task simple and short at first and gradually work your way upward. This helps teach your child to concentrate even though there are distractions around her.

You can teach children to listen with a similar game. You say something to them and they have to repeat back the essence of what you said. Teaching them to maintain eye contact while listening is also helpful. Again, a star or reward is appropriate.

Find opportunities to praise your child in the course of ordinary, everyday events. If, for instance, you notice your child deliberating over which color to use in her drawing, praise her for taking the time to think about it.

Use everyday opportunities too, to model for your child the thoughtful as opposed to the hasty approach. When shopping, for instance, think out loud about the advantages of one product over another as you make your choice.

The importance of praise and appropriate rewards cannot be stressed enough. Children need to feel competent and proud of themselves. Praise or reward for even a small amount of change will enhance the child's confidence and encourage her to strive for even greater change.

*annie story*

Annie was a little girl who lived in a brown brick house with her mommy and her daddy and a big black dog.[1]

One day Annie came home from school very upset.

"What's the matter, Annie?" her mom asked when she saw Annie's face.

"I got my homework wrong again," said Annie. "The teacher was really mad at me. She said I should have known the answers and that I had to do better next time."

"Did you know the answers?" asked Annie's mom.

"Well, it was funny," said Annie, "but when she showed them to me, I knew I did know them."

"What do you think happened?" asked her mom.

"The teacher said I must have rushed through the homework so fast that I didn't take time to think properly."

"Well, you do tend to jump right into things," said her mom, "and when you do that, you don't give yourself a chance to think."

Annie looked miserable. "But I can't help it," she said. "I always do that. I'm just like that."

"Lots of kids are like that," said her mom, "but there is something that can be done. There is a way you can change."

"Really?" said Annie. "I could really change?" It would be so good to change, she thought to herself. It would mean that she wouldn't always be getting into trouble for rushing in and giving the wrong answers or for yelling out an answer when the class was supposed to be thinking.[2]

Her mom nodded. "Yes, there is a way you can change," she said. "Would you like me to show you how?"

"I sure would," said Annie.

---

[1] Change the details to suit your child.
[2] Children need to be motivated to change.

"Okay," said her mom. "First we have to teach you how to listen to your brain properly. You have the most fantastic, terrific brain in there, but you're not taking the time to listen to it."

"Really?" said Annie. "I have a fantastic, terrific brain?"[3]

"You certainly have," said her mom. "And I think you're going to get a nice surprise when you find out how well you can listen to it and use it."

"Great," said Annie. "How do I do it?"

"Why don't you get me last night's homework," said her mom, "and I'll show you how to do it so that you're giving your brain a chance to do its work properly."

"Okay," said Annie and she went and got her homework.

"Now," said her mom, "just watch while I do this problem. I'm going to talk to myself so that you can see just how I do it and what my brain is thinking." She took the homework question and looked at it.[4]

"Okay," she said. "Now, first of all, what am I supposed to be doing?" She looked at the homework question again. "I see," she said, "I'm supposed to look at these four pictures and figure out which one doesn't belong. First I'll look at each picture, one by one, and see what it's about. One is a picture of a tiger. The next one is a picture of an elephant. The next is a picture of a zebra. The last one is a picture of a dog. Let's see, which one is different from the others? I think it's the zebra because the zebra's striped. Whoops, no, the tiger has stripes too, so the zebra isn't the odd one out. I know, the tiger, the elephant, and the zebra are all wild animals, but the dog isn't. The dog must be the odd one out. Hey, that was good thinking. I'm pleased with myself."

"Gee," said Annie, "that was neat. Could I do that?"

"Sure," said her mom. "Let's write down the things I did so you can remember them."[5]

---

[3]Letting children know this boosts their self-esteem as well as their confidence, both of which will help them in mastering the new changes.

[4]It is extremely helpful to first model the self-talk behavior yourself. Children find it easier to learn a new behavior when they see it demonstrated rather than just hearing it described.

[5]Writing the steps down helps your child remember them.

"Here's some paper," said Annie. "Can I write it?"

"Sure," said her mom. "Now, the first thing I had to do was find out what the problem was."

"You mean you had to say what the teacher wanted you to do," said Annie.

"That's right," said her mom. "How shall we write that down?"[6]

"Let's put this," said Annie, and she wrote down: "1. Find out what you're supposed to be doing."

"Okay," said her mom. "Now, the next thing I had to do was find out how to go about doing it. What I did was to go slowly and look at all the choices. What will we put for that?"

"I know, said Annie, and she wrote: "2. Work out how to do it. Go slowly. Look at all the choices."

"Great," said her mom. "Sometimes it's also a good idea to remind yourself to concentrate, so why don't we put that in."

So Annie wrote: "3. Concentrate and think only about what I'm doing."

"Very good," said her mom. "Now, the next thing I had to do was pick the answer."

Annie wrote: "4. Find the answer."

"And then," said her mom, "I remembered to tell myself that I'd worked well and done a good job."

"I like that part," said Annie. And she wrote: "5. Tell myself I did a good job.

"What if I got the answer wrong, though?" she asked her mom. "What should I say then?"

"Well," said her mom, "one of the things you *don't* say is, 'I got the answer wrong—that means I'm a dummy,' because that's not true. If you get an answer wrong, you can just say, 'Uh-oh, that answer was wrong. I'll just have to think about it again.'"[7]

"That sounds okay," said Annie, and she wrote it down on her piece of paper so that she would remember it.

---

[6]Use your child's phraseology, not your own.

[7]It is important to teach your child how to deal appropriately with failures. Rather than berating herself into hopelessness, the child learns to say, "I made a mistake, but I'll do better next time."

"Can I do a problem now?" she asked her mom.

"Okay," said her mom, pointing to Annie's homework book. "Why don't you do this one?"

Annie looked at her piece of paper.

"Okay," she said to herself, "first I have to figure out what I'm supposed to be doing."[8]

She looked at the problem. "I'm supposed to find which two things go together out of these six pictures."

Then she said, "Next, I have to go slowly and look at all the choices. Let's see, there's six pictures—a teacup, a frying pan, an egg cup, a tea kettle, a fork, and a salt shaker."

She looked at all the pictures. Then she said to herself, "I have to concentrate on this and work out the answer. Let's see, the egg cup and the teacup both have cups in their name, but no, I don't really think they go together. I know what the answer is—it's the teacup and the tea kettle. They both go together. That was good thinking. I'm pleased with myself."

"That was terrific," said her mom. "You did that really well."

"That was neat," said Annie. "Can I do another one?"

"Sure thing," said her mom.

"I'm going to do all my homework like this," said Annie.

"That's a great idea," said her mom.

Annie nodded.[9]


"You know," said Annie's mom, "I thought of something else that can help you slow down and give your brain a chance to think properly."

"What's that?" asked Annie. She was interested.

"It's called relaxation," said her mom. "Do you want me to show you how to do it?"

Annie nodded. She was looking forward to this.

"Well," said her mom, "when you're relaxed, the muscles in your

---

[8]After you have demonstrated the technique, let your child run through it. She should talk out loud. This helps you check that she is following the steps correctly and also helps her learn the steps.

[9]You can pause here if you want to tell the story in sections.

body are all loose and floppy like this." And she held out her arm and made it go all loose and floppy and drop down to her lap. "A good way of getting your muscles floppy is to squeeze them really tight and then just let them go so that they're like a floppy rag doll. Why don't we do that together?"

"Okay," said Annie.

"Let's start with one arm," said her mom.

So they squeezed their arm muscles really tight, as tight as they could, and then they let their arms flop and plop, like sacks of potatoes, onto their laps.

"Great," said Annie's mom.

"This is fun," said Annie.

"Let's go through all the muscles in our bodies," said her mom.

So they relaxed their other arms, their chest muscles, their tummies, their back muscles, their leg muscles, their neck muscles, and all of the muscles all over their bodies until they were loose and floppy all over.

"That feels good," said Annie. "I like that feeling."

"It is a nice feeling," said her mom.[10]

"Now," said Annie's mom, "while you're all nice and relaxed, you might like to imagine yourself doing all the things we've talked about. You can imagine yourself taking time to think and work things out. You can feel how good that feels."

So Annie imagined herself doing her work step by step.

"It does feel good," said Annie. "I like being able to stop and think. It makes me feel like I know what I'm doing."

"Imagining things is a very special way to practice," said Annie's mom, "and it will help you feel like you know what you're doing in real life."

The next day Annie came home from school beaming. "Look," she said to her mom, "I got all my homework right!"

"That's fantastic, Annie," said her mom, and she gave her a big hug.

"What I wondered, though," said Annie, "was what I do when

---

[10]If you want to go further with the relaxation, see Chapter 14.

I have to do problems in class. It looks weird to talk out loud to yourself in class."

"That's a good point," said Annie's mom. "What you do is, you still use the five things you wrote down on your card, but instead of saying them out loud, you whisper them. Then after a while, you won't even need to whisper them. You can just say them silently to yourself. Look, I'll show you how and then we can practice."

"This is great," said Annie. "Boy, is my teacher going to get a shock when she sees what I can really do!"[11]

A few weeks later, Annie came home from school looking unhappy.

"What's wrong, Annie?" asked her mom.

"I got into trouble with my teacher again," said Annie. "It's not my schoolwork. She said she's really pleased with that. It's Mary. Mary got me into a fight, and my teacher got really mad at me."

"I can see that that's upset you," said her mom. "Why don't you tell me what happened, and we'll see what we can do about it?"

"Well," said Annie, "it happened at lunchtime. Mary was in this weird mood and she kept saying silly things to me. I got upset and yelled at her, then we got into a fight, and then I got into trouble."

"Well," said her mom, "I think there's something we can do to help with that sort of situation."

"What?" said Annie. She was really curious. She couldn't imagine what it could be.

"Well," said her mom, "let's just think first. You said Mary was saying silly things to you. What do you think she wanted you to do?"[12]

Annie thought for a moment. "I think she wanted to stir me up—to get me mad."

"That sounds right," said her mom. "And you did just what she wanted you to."

---

[11]One section of the story ends here. You may pause before proceeding with the next section.

[12]Questions like this help your child analyze and think through problems.

"Gosh," said Annie. "I never thought of it like that." She shook her head. "I don't like that idea. I don't want to go around getting mad just because Mary wants me to."[13]

"No," said her mom. "I didn't think you would. And besides, most people don't like to go around feeling mad and getting into trouble. It just doesn't feel good."

"Well, what can I do about it?" asked Annie.

"Remember how you learned to listen to your brain when you were doing homework problems?" asked Annie's mom.

Annie nodded.

"Well, you can do the same sort of thing with this," said Mom.

"How?" asked Annie

"Well," said her mom, "the first thing is to give yourself time to think instead of jumping right in and saying or doing something."[14]

Annie nodded. "And I know what to do next," she said. "I have to find out what the problem is."

"That's right," said her mom. "That's very good."

"I think," said Annie, "that the problem is that Mary's saying silly things to me and I'm feeling angry."

"That sounds right," said her mom. "Why don't we think of a few things you could do about it?"

"I could yell at her to be quiet," said Annie.

"Yes," said her mom, "that's one thing."

"I could tell the teacher on her," said Annie.

"Yes," said her mom, "that's a second thing you could do."

"I could not pay any attention to her," said Annie.

"That's right," said her mom. "That's a third thing you could do. Why don't you write all those things down on a piece of paper?"

"Okay," said Annie, and she did.

"Now," said her mom. "Step 1 was to stop, think, and see what the problem was. Step 2 was to write down some different things

---

[13]Most children don't like the idea of playing into their opponent's hand. This gives them added incentive to avoid being sucked into the other person's game.

[14]These steps run parallel to the five problem-solving steps Annie used in the first part of the story.

you could do about the problem. For step 3 we have to decide which of those things is the best thing to do."

"How do we do that?" asked Annie.

"Well, let's see what would have happened with each of those three choices, then we'll be able to tell which is the best choice. Why don't we start with yelling at Mary to be quiet? What would have happened if you'd done that?"

Annie thought. "I don't think it would have made any difference. I think she would have kept saying those things. Then probably I would yell at her more and we'd get into a fight."

"Okay," said Annie's mom. "What do you think would have happened if you'd told the teacher?"

"Well, the teacher might have told Mary to stop. But I think I'd feel sort of funny having to tell the teacher—like I was a baby or something."

"Okay," said her mom. "Now what would have happened if you'd ignored Mary?"

"Well," said Annie. "I guess I would have walked right past her and not paid any attention to her. Then she wouldn't have been able to get me into a fight."

"Well," said Annie's mom, "now that you've thought all that out, which is the best solution to your problem?"

Annie thought for a moment. "To walk straight past her," she said. "That would have been the best thing to do."

"Can you think of anything that might make it easier for you to ignore Mary's teasing and walk right past her?"

Annie thought. "I guess I could talk to myself like I do when I'm solving problems."

"What could you say to yourself?" asked Annie's mom.

"I could say something like, 'Cool down. Mary's just trying to get me mad. She'd like me to get mad and get into trouble. I'm going to walk right past her and not pay any attention. I'm not going to get tricked by her into getting mad. I'll feel much more pleased with myself if I just stay cool and don't pay any attention."[15]

---

[15]Here Annie is using "self-talk" to help her keep her cool.

"That's very good, Annie," said her mom. "You did a great job." Then she paused and said, "I have a good idea. To give you some practice at this, why don't I pretend to be Mary? I'll say silly things to you, and you can practice ignoring me and telling yourself all those things you just said."[16]

"Okay," said Annie, "that sounds like fun."

So her mom pretended to be Mary and teased and called Annie names.

Annie just walked past without paying any attention. She felt very pleased with herself.

"That was great," she said to her mom. "Can we do it again?"

"Sure," said her mom.

So they did.

"This is terrific," said Annie. "Now that I know what to do, things are going to be much easier at school. And I can use it for all sorts of things."[17]

"That's right," said her mom. "All you need to do is do what you just did then—take time to think, work out the things you could do and what would happen if you did them, and then pick the best choice. You also know how to talk yourself through things to help you keep cool and make the right choices."

"You know what?" said Annie. "It feels good when you take the time to let your brain think." She tapped on her head. "You were right, you know," she said. "I think I do have a pretty good brain up here."

"You certainly do," said her mom and she gave Annie a great big hug.

---

[16]Role-playing is an excellent way for children to get practice at staying calm in the face of taunting or teasing.

[17]Let your child know that this method can be applied to all sorts of problems. Pick some out to practice solving with her.

# 12

## Siblings

Imagine how you would feel if the government suddenly decreed that a huge lottery was going to be held. You were to pull a number out of a barrel, and the owner of that ticket was to come and live with you—to share your house, income, food, and family for life. You were to have no choice in the matter and no way of prearranging which number you drew. This is not the sort of scenario that most people would greet with cries of rapture. And yet, this is exactly what many of us have already experienced—it happens with the birth of a baby brother or sister.

The introduction of a new baby into the family is a crucial time, and I've dealt with this in the first book of Annie Stories. This story is set at a later date when the new baby is no longer a baby. She is now old enough to play with her sister. She is also old enough to fight.

Fighting is something that most siblings do with great gusto and often great frequency. They are in competition for space, possessions, achievements, individual identities, and parental love and attention. They may be totally different in personality and yet be forced to live together in a relationship far closer than friendship. Try as they may, there is no escape from this relationship. Is it any wonder that conflicts are common?

Perhaps the astonishing thing about sibling relationships is not that they contain so much negativity, but that so many siblings are able to touch their relationships with the Philosophers' Stone, that magical substance that alchemists believed was able to turn base metal into gold. Out of the darker emotions of jealousy, greed, fear, and anger, siblings can bring forth altruism, generosity, supportiveness, and love.

Such a transformation does not happen magically, of course. It

179

requires time and effort on the part of the siblings, and support and understanding on the part of the parents.

Parents can help by giving each child a firm and loving sense of her special place in the family and in their affections. The more secure each child feels, the easier she will find it to resolve the conflicts of siblinghood.

Parents often put a lot of pressure on children by insisting that they love each other and refusing to acknowledge any other emotion: "She is your *sister*," "He's the only brother you've got," and so on. The child's reaction to this may be, "Well, I wish he/she wasn't."

Siblings don't choose each other. With luck, your sibling may be someone you would have picked as a friend anyway. But often, in fact, your sibling is someone you would never have picked as a friend. Even with the most companionable of siblings, there will still be elements of competition, envy, and rivalry. With less friendly siblings, the situation is even more strife-ridden.

It is natural that siblings at times experience emotions such as rage, hatred, and frustration. Insisting that they don't doesn't make it true. It simply makes the feelings go underground. They are then fueled by the extra burden of resentment, by the sense of being misunderstood, and by possible guilt or fear at the intensity of their "forbidden" feelings. Often, when the bad feelings go underground, so do the genuine good feelings. What emerges instead may be something like an armed neutrality, a polite hostility, or a forced sweetness that is patently false.

Recognize that your children may have intense negative feelings about each other at times. Encourage your children to find a way of expressing these feelings that tones down their impact. For instance, if your children commonly express negative feelings by beating each other up, encourage them to use words instead of fists. If they habitually hurl verbal abuse at each other, encourage them to write the words down on a "Complaint Form" rather than scream them. Show them how to punch pillows rather than each other, to scribble their anger out onto drawing paper, to kick a ball around the yard, and so on. Often it is not until the bad feelings have come out that the good feelings can be spontaneously expressed.

Parents can help children deal with the complexities of sibling relationships in several ways.

They can acknowledge that each of their children is unique. They can respect each child's need for private space and possessions. Personal possessions are important to children; they are part of their sense of identity, and it can be very upsetting to them if siblings are constantly taking or damaging their special things. You wouldn't like it if your neighbor kept taking your car and forgetting to bring it back or leaving the headlights on all night. Insist that children ask permission before borrowing or playing with each other's possessions. This saves the owner from feeling in constant danger of being invaded and robbed.

Children need to know they are loved and valued as individuals. They do not need to be treated in exactly the same way—they are not exactly the same people. What is right for one will be wrong for the other. They do need to feel, however, that they are each being treated fairly.

Fairly does not necessarily mean equally. Children have different needs at different times; focus on meeting the needs of the individual child at the appropriate time. For instance, one may need a new dress to go to a special party. This doesn't have to mean that the other child gets a new dress, too. Sometime later that other child may need a new tennis racquet. At that time, she will be the one getting the treat rather than her sister. Aim to treat each child according to her individual requirements rather than as just part of a duo, trio, or quartet.

It is generally more helpful for parents to avoid the role of judge and jury in the resolution of children's fights. Many fights are staged at some level to gain your attention. If you buy into that, you complete a triangle, and triangles are notoriously difficult to resolve. Instead, when conflicts come up, you can teach your children conflict-resolution techniques to help them resolve their clashes.

When we're involved in an argument, many of us are convinced that the other person just hasn't heard or understood the point we're making. We figure that if we can just say it loudly enough, forcefully enough, and often enough, that will remedy their deafness. It usually doesn't—they're so busy plotting their defense against our perceived attack that they don't have a chance to really listen. Yet, once we feel we have been genuinely heard, we feel much less need to shout.

The first step is to allow each child to state her grievance while the other child listens. Encourage each child to summarize her sibling's position to make sure she has listened properly and understood. When each child has recapped what the other was saying, let them sum up what the core of the conflict is. For example, "There is only one toy bunny but we both want to play with it."

Next, encourage the children to make a list of possible solutions to the conflict, making it clear that neither of them will be able to play with the bunny until they can both agree on a solution.

If they don't come up with an agreed solution, take the problem to a "family council." This is a meeting at which all of the family is present and everyone brainstorms together to come up with a workable compromise.

Although sibling relationships do contain the seeds of destructive emotions, they can also provide the challenge that enables children to resolve their conflicts and rise above them in the creation of loving and lasting bonds. They can teach children how to cope with the various hurdles that life will set in their way, such as losing, fighting, and envying, and how to become stronger through coping with them.

## *annie story*

Annie was a little girl who lived in a brown brick house with her mommy and her daddy and a big black dog. Someone else lived in the house too—Annie's little sister, Cynthia.[1]

Right now Annie was wishing Cynthia didn't live in the house. Annie was wishing Cynthia had never been born. Annie was wishing that Cynthia was a piece of doggy-doo that was just about to get stepped on, or a toad that was so ugly that people ran away

---

[1]Change the details to suit your child.

and screamed when they saw it, or a block of ice on the sidewalk on a very, very hot day, or a piece of secondhand toilet paper, or . . . Annie's brain had run out of things to wish that Cynthia was. So she just scowled at her instead.

"It's not fair," said Cynthia. "It's my turn to play with Bobo." She reached out and grabbed the toy bunny.

"Is not," said Annie and snatched Bobo back.

"Is!" yelled Cynthia.

"Is not!" yelled Annie.

"Is!"

"Is not!"

"Children!" said their mother. She had just come in the door and stood holding her hands to her ears. "There's the most terrible noise coming from somewhere in this house. People have been calling on the phone from miles away to ask what it is. All over town the cats and the dogs are trying to crawl under the beds. Someone even called the local TV station to say that World War III had started. What on earth could be happening?"[2]

Annie smiled slightly.

Cynthia giggled.

"I can't imagine what could be going on" said Mom.

"It was us," said Annie.

"We were having a fight," said Cynthia.

"Oh," said mom. "What were you having a fight about?"

Cynthia pointed at Bobo. "Annie won't let me play with him."

"She tried to grab him from me!" said Annie. "I hadn't finished playing with him."

"Annie's being mean!" said Cynthia. "I hate her."

"Cynthia's being a pest!" said Annie. "I hate her."

"I get the feeling," said Annie's mom looking at them, "that you're both pretty mad at each other."

"You bet," said Cynthia and made a face at Annie. "Pigface!" she said.

"Creep!" said Annie and made a face back.

"I think it's time to cool off for a minute," said Annie's mom.

---

[2]A touch of humor can help defuse tensions.

"Come into the living room with me, and let's sit down. I have a story that I think you might be interested in."

Annie followed her mom into the living room. Cynthia followed a few steps behind her. Annie was sure that Cynthia was making faces at her behind her back.

Annie's mom settled herself on the couch between Annie and Cynthia. "Once upon a time," she said, "there was a little girl called Andrea. Andrea lived with her mommy and her daddy in a brown brick house with a big black dog. Another person lived in the house, too. That was Andrea's sister, Celia.[3] Andrea loved living in her house, but she didn't like living with Celia. If Andrea was playing a game, Celia would come and interrupt. If Celia wanted to play with one of Andrea's toys, she would just take it. Sometimes, even worse, she would break it. Celia wanted to have her way *all* the time. Celia called Andrea names and said mean things to her. Sometimes Celia would pinch or poke Andrea or say nasty things to her until a fight started. Sometimes Andrea got blamed for the things Celia did. Andrea felt really mad about that. But worst of all, when Andrea wanted to have some time with Mommy or Daddy just for her, Celia was always there. And even worse than the worst of all was that Andrea knew that deep down, Mommy and Daddy really liked Celia better than they liked Andrea. She could tell this because Mom and Dad never got as mad at Celia as they did at Andrea. They were nicer to Celia than they were to Andrea. They paid Celia lots more attention than they did Andrea. They let Celia get away with things that they would never let Andrea get away with. When Andrea was in trouble, they were meaner to her than they were to Celia. When Andrea thought about it, she got really mad. It just wasn't fair. It wasn't fair. It wasn't fair at all!"[4]

Annie's mother stopped for a minute. Annie and Cynthia were both listening goggle-eyed.

---

[3]If you're telling this story to two children at once, it's helpful to choose names that are similar to both of theirs. This allows each child to see herself as the focus of the story.

[4]It is common for children to experience themselves as being unfairly treated in comparison to their sibling.

"Hey," said Annie, "I'd like to meet Andrea. We'd have lots to talk about. She sounds just like me!"

"What do you mean?" said Cynthia. "She sounds just like me!" Annie looked at her. "But if she's like me, she can't be like you."

"Well, she is like me," said Cynthia. "I feel just like she does about her sister."

"Well, I feel just like she does about her sister," said Annie. They stared at each other.

"That's weird," said Annie.

"I never knew you felt just like me," said Cynthia.

"Well, I never knew you felt just like me," said Annie.[5]

They looked at each other for a while longer.

"Well, girls," said their mom, "do you want to hear the rest of the story?"

"Sure," said Annie.

Cynthia nodded.

"One day," Mom continued, "Andrea was playing with her favorite toy, Dozy. Dozy was a stuffed toy puppy with long floppy ears. Celia was sitting in the room watching Andrea play.

"'Hey,' said Celia. 'You've been playing with Dozy for ages. I want to play with Dozy. It's my turn to play with Dozy.'

"'No,' said Andrea, 'I'm playing with Dozy.'

"'It's not fair!' said Celia. 'I want Dozy.'

"'Well, you can't have him,' said Andrea.

"'Can so!' said Celia, and she grabbed Dozy.

"'Give him back, you little creep!' said Andrea, and she grabbed Dozy back.

"'I want him!' said Celia. 'You're a big mean pig!' And she burst into tears.

"Suddenly their mother appeared in the doorway. 'Girls! Girls!' she said. 'What's going on here? I've never heard so much noise in my life.'

"Celia pointed at Dozy. 'Andrea won't let me play with him. It's not fair!'

---

[5]It can be enlightening for siblings to recognize that they have similar feelings and perceptions.

"'She tried to grab him from me,' said Andrea. 'I hadn't finished playing with him. It's not fair!'

"'Well,' said their mom, 'I can see you're both pretty mad at each other. It looks like you both wanted to play with Dozy at the same time and that was a problem for you.'[6]

"Andrea and Celia nodded.

"'But,' Mom went on, 'I'm sure it's a problem you can solve.[7] Hang on for a minute, I'm just going into the other room to get something.'

"Andrea and Celia looked at each other. What on earth was Mom going to get?

"Mom was back in a moment. 'Here you are,' she said and handed Andrea and Celia a large writing pad and a pencil. 'I want you to sit down and work out seven[8] ways to solve your problem. They have to be ways that you can both agree on. You can write them down on this pad. When you've written them down, come and call me. I'll be in the other room. With Dozy,' she added as she picked up the toy puppy and headed for the door. 'I'm really looking forward to seeing what you two come up with. I bet it will be terrific.'

"Andrea and Celia looked at each other.

"'I guess we'd better do it,' said Andrea.

"'I guess so,' said Celia. 'Otherwise no one will get to play with Dozy.'

"'Hmmm,' said Andrea.

"'Hmmm,' said Celia.

"And they started to think.

"'I know,' said Andrea, 'we could make a rule that Dozy is mine to play with and no one else could touch him.'

"'No,' said Celia. 'That's not fair to me. I wouldn't agree to it, and Mommy said we both have to agree to it.'

"'Okay,' said Andrea, 'we won't put that down then.'

---

[6]Stating the problem clearly helps the children to go on to find a solution.

[7]This positive response, which indicates confidence in the children's ability to find a solution, is much more helpful than a negative one along the lines of "You're always fighting, you two are hopeless, you never learn," etc. Children labeled as competent are much more likely to find a solution than those labeled as incompetent.

[8]The figure seven is rather arbitrary. The number will depend somewhat on the concentration span and age of your children.

"'I've got an idea,' said Celia. 'We could cut Dozy in half and then we'd each have half.'

"Andrea wrinkled her nose, but she wrote that down under number 1.

"'I've got another good idea,' said Celia. 'We could get Mommy to buy another Dozy and then we could each have one.'

"'I like that idea,' said Andrea, 'but I don't think Mom will.'

"'Let's write it down anyway,' said Celia.

"So Andrea wrote it down and put the number 2 next to it. 'Now we have to think of five more,' she said. She thought for a while.

"'I've got another idea,' she said. 'We could put a bad-smell spell on Dozy, then neither of us would want to play with him.'

"'We wouldn't have to put a bad-smell spell on Dozy,' said Celia. 'All we'd have to do is drop him in the toilet.'[9]

"Andrea rolled around laughing.

"'How many have we got so far?' said Celia.

"'Three,' said Andrea. 'We have four more to go.'

"'We could play another game and forget about Dozy,' said Andrea.

"'Okay,' said Celia, 'that can be number 4.'

"'We could take turns playing with Dozy,' said Celia. 'We could time ourselves with that special clock Mommy has in the kitchen. The one that has a very loud ring.'

"'We could toss a coin to see who got first turn,' said Andrea. 'If it came down heads, I would play with Dozy first and if it came down tails, you would.'

"'That makes number 5,' said Celia. 'We need two more.'

"'I could let you play with Dozy in return for you letting me play with your new paint set,' said Andrea.

"'How many's that?' asked Celia.

"'Six,' said Andrea. 'We've got one more to go.' She thought for a minute. 'I know,' she said, 'we could pretend that we were puppy dogs, too, like Dozy, and then we could all three play games together. That makes seven.'

---

[9]Some humor lightens the atmosphere. You might encourage your children to include some of the weirdest solutions they can think of as well as the most sensible.

"'Great,' said Celia, 'let's go and tell Mom.'

"'That's terrific,' said their mom as she looked at the list. 'Now all you have to do is pick the best one and your problem's solved.'

"'Neat,' said Andrea and she and Celia put their heads together.

"They whispered for a few minutes and then, 'We've picked one,' said Celia.[10]

"'Yes,' said Andrea. 'We've picked number 5. That's the one about taking turns.'

"'So we'll need your special clock to time ourselves with,' said Celia. She loved playing with the clock.

"'Sure thing,' said their mom. 'You know, I'm really proud of you two.' And she gave them both a great big hug."

"Hey," said Annie, "that was a great story."

"Do you think that we could do that too?" asked Cynthia. "I mean, make a list of seven ways to solve our problem?"

"You bet," said Mommy.

"Let's do it now," said Annie. "Could you get us some paper and pencils?" she said to Mommy.

"I certainly can," said her mom, and she found some paper and pencils.

"Now, the first thing you need to do," she said, "before starting your list is to decide what the problem is. Each of you might have a different idea about what the problem is. So you could take turns to say what you think the problem is. While you're saying it, the other person has to listen very carefully and then repeat it back to make sure they've heard it right.[11] Then you can write it down and start making your list of seven ways to solve it."

"Great," said Annie. She picked up the pencil.

"Let's do it," said Cynthia and they sat down to solve their problem.

---

[10]Having the children pick a solution enhances the possibility that they will stick to it. It also builds up feelings of competence and autonomy.

[11]This is a very useful step. It ensures that each child feels listened to and heard rather than shouted over.

# 13
# Children of Alcoholics

The incidence of alcoholism is staggering. Some studies suggest that there is an alcoholic home in the background of more than 10 percent of the population of the USA. This means that there are currently between 25 million and 28 million children of alcoholics living in America.

Despite these extraordinary figures, one of the parado.·es of living with an alcoholic is that it is often perceived by the family as something that sets them apart from the rest of the community, a shameful secret to be kept so that people won't guess that they are different. The knowledge that there are so many people carrying a similar secret and living in similar conditions can come as a huge relief. This is particularly so for children, who usually hate being different from their friends and peers.

The alcoholism of one member invariably affects the whole family. Often the husband or wife of the alcoholic is stretched to the limit in trying to deal with the stresses and strains involved. Spouses of alcoholics are often caught up in inadequate or inappropriate ways of coping. They often try to deny that the problem exists or attempt to cover it up to protect the children. Often they give confused messages to the children—telling them, for instance, that nothing is wrong, but that they are not allowed to tell anyone about it. They may overprotect the children or neglect them. Often they rely on the children for emotional support, which forces the children to grow up too fast.

Not only is it forbidden to talk about alcoholism outside the family, but it is usually a forbidden subject within the family. Children are thus left confused, frightened, and helpless. They know something is very wrong, but they are not allowed to talk about it or told that it is nothing. They are denied a stable relationship with the alcoholic parent but may have difficulties in relating to the nonalcoholic parent due to the conspiracy of silence and the stressed preoccupation of that parent. They may feel emotionally isolated within the family. Furthermore, as they are encouraged to be wary of forming ties outside the family (because of the "secret"), they may never develop the stable, trusting contacts that are essential for their emotional growth.

Along with the alcoholism, there is often verbal or physical violence within the family. This is of great concern to most children, who worry about themselves or other family members being hurt. Some studies show that children consider the fighting in the home to be worse than the drinking it accompanies.

The children of alcoholics are generally beset by many doubts and fears. They may worry about the health of the alcoholic parent. They may be confused by the intensity and the ambivalence of their feelings toward that parent—they may both love and hate him or her. They may be constantly thrown off balance by the inconsistency and unpredictability of the alcoholic parent's behavior. They may be hurt and angry that they cannot rely on more support from the nonalcoholic parent. They may feel betrayed and unloved. They may feel responsible for their parent's drinking.

In all of this, they are likely to feel unusually helpless and powerless. Because of the shame and emphasis on secrecy, they feel cut off from outside help. They may have absorbed the message that people are untrustworthy and unpredictable. They have often learned to avoid the expression and even the awareness of feelings. Low self-esteem is common.

Many children cope by becoming wary, tightly controlled individuals. They see themselves as mature and responsible. They distrust spontaneity and constantly monitor their own and others' behavior and reactions. They try to separate themselves as much as possible from contact with their family. They feel powerless and worthless and are highly critical of themselves. They may have an excessive need to seek approval and affirmation.

Some studies have identified different types of reactions to an alcoholic parent. Sharon Wegscheider sees four different coping styles. The "hero" is a child who takes on a super-responsible role in the family, taking charge of chores and organizational tasks. The "scape-goat" is the focus for family frustrations and conflicts. The "lost child" has a very poor sense of identity, finds it hard to know where she fits into the family, and keeps a very low profile. The "mascot" is often the baby of the family and may be cosseted and overprotected.

Claudia Black has also described several roles which she feels children of alcoholics commonly fall into. The "delinquent" or "acting-out" child is similar to Wegscheider's "scape-goat." The "responsible" child corresponds to the "hero." Black also talks about the "adjuster" who basically copes with the chaos by ignoring it. This child has some similarities to the "lost child." Lastly, Black talks about the "placater." The placater tries to smooth people's feelings and make them happy or at least not quarrelsome. She works hard at pleasing people. This child is somewhat similar to the "mascot."

All of these children are coping at a cost to themselves. The cost is often that of emotional impoverishment, problematic relationships, and low self-esteem.

As well as the above roles, another group, called the "invulnerables," has been identified. These children manage to surmount their family problem and grow into healthy, well-functioning adults.

Studies show that children who are able to establish good, solid relationships outside the home are not as likely to become alcoholics as those who are unable to do this. People or institutions that the child connects with in a positive way can provide a vitally important source of support and nourishment for the child. They can give the child a sense of direction, a role model, and a sense of belonging that has a marked effect on the child's sense of self-esteem and well-being.

Another important factor is the nonalcoholic parents. Although they may feel helpless to alleviate their children's pain and distress, their role in fact can be powerfully beneficial. One study found that the main difference between adult children of alcoholics who were now doing well, as compared to those who were not, was that the ones who were doing well all had a very positive image of how their nonalcoholic parent fulfilled his or her role as a parent.

As the spouse of an alcoholic, you may find it painful to read the following Annie Story. It is important, however, to remember that your input can make a real and enormously positive difference to your child.

Asking for outside help is a very important first step for the families of alcoholics. It involves coming out into the open and breaking the code of secrecy, but it is an essential move in the journey towards a healthier and happier life. Help can come from many areas; self-help groups such as Alcoholics Anonymous and Al Anon, counselors, teachers, psychologists, doctors, social workers, psychiatrists, family therapists, and drug and alcohol counselors are all important sources of help. Such people can assist the family in dealing with its difficulties. They can also work with the children to bolster their self-esteem, help them develop and maintain healthy relationships, and allow them to feel comfortable expressing and exploring their feelings.

## *annie story*

Annie was a little girl who lived in a brown brick house with her mommy and her daddy and a big black dog.[1]

One day Annie was at school. Her teacher, Mrs. Rowan, was talking to the class about the new project. They were going to create a class newspaper. All of the kids had written articles for the newspaper and now Mrs. Rowan was going to announce who would be the editor of the newspaper. The editor was in charge of deciding which articles to print and how to arrange them.

Mrs. Rowan looked around the classroom.

"I have decided," she said, "that there will be two editors for the class newspaper. The editors will be Annie and Sally."

---

[1]Change the details to suit your child.

Annie and Sally looked at each other and gave each other big grins. Annie was very excited. She thought she might like to be a writer when she grew up. Being editor of the class newspaper seemed like a good start.

After school Sally said to Annie, "We'd better get together and pick out what articles we'll use for the class paper."

"Great," said Annie. She was looking forward to this.

"Why don't we go to your house," said Sally.

Annie's smile disappeared. "N-no!" she said. "We can't go to my house."[2]

Sally looked surprised. "Why not?" she asked. "I haven't ever been to your house."

Annie searched wildly for something to say. She couldn't think of anything. "Uh, we just can't go there today," she said.

"Oh, well," said Sally, "I guess we'd better go to my house then."

Annie felt miserable. Sally must think she was awful. She probably thought Annie was weird.[3] Well, she was right. Most of the time Annie felt weird. Weird and awful. She wished she could have invited Sally home to her house, like all the other, normal kids did. But Annie couldn't. Because Annie had a secret. She wasn't a normal kid. She wasn't a normal kid with a normal family.

Annie had a father who drank. Most of the time when her father was around, he was drunk. When he was drunk, his voice would get louder, a lot louder. He would rant and rave and yell and sometimes throw things at whoever was in his way. And someone was always in his way. Annie was terrified of him when he was drunk. She would run and hide or try to get out of the house. But often she wasn't quick enough. Annie was terrified that if she brought one of her friends home, her father might come in drunk and start yelling and screaming and acting like a crazy person. Annie thought that if that happened, she would just die on the spot. She would be so ashamed that she couldn't stand it. So she never

---

[2]Children of alcoholics are often scared to invite friends home.
[3]Children of alcoholics often think of themselves as abnormal—set apart from the rest because of their family background.

brought anyone home. It made it harder to make friends when you couldn't ask people over to your house, but Annie figured it was better not to make friends than to risk having a friend see her father when he was drunk.[4]

When Annie's father wasn't drunk, he was like a different person. You could talk to him and ask him things and he would answer you properly, like a normal person. Sometimes he even played games with Annie or read her stories. Annie liked her father when he wasn't drunk, but when he was drunk, she hated him.[5]

Sometimes when Annie's father wasn't drunk, he would promise to do fun things with her. But when he got drunk, he would forget the promises and yell at Annie instead. Annie really hated those times. And after a while it got so that she never trusted anything he said. What was the use of getting excited about his promises when all that happened was that he got drunk and forgot them? Annie decided it was much better not to get her hopes up.[6] She thought that if her dad really loved her, he would keep his promises and he wouldn't drink so much. She thought her dad didn't really love her at all.[7]

Annie tried to get her mom to help, but her mom didn't even want to talk about it.

"There's nothing wrong," Annie's mom would say. And then in the next breath she would add, "And don't you tell anyone about this."[8]

Annie thought that was pretty weird. If there was nothing wrong, why shouldn't she tell anyone?

Annie's mom always looked worried and unhappy. Often she snapped at Annie. Sometimes Annie would catch her crying.

---

[4]The experience of being humiliated or abused in front of friends is a very painful one for most children.

[5]Children often have ambivalent feelings toward the alcoholic parent. The parent may seem to take on two totally different personas—one when drunk and one when sober.

[6]Often children react to this situation by simply not expecting anything. This means that as well as giving up their disappointments, they also give up their hopes.

[7]It is common for children to feel this.

[8]This is a very confusing statement for children to hear. On the one hand it admits that something is wrong, while on the other hand it denies it.

Annie felt bad when that happened. She felt sorry for her mom and she wished there were something she could do to make her happy. But sometimes Annie felt angry at her mom and thought that she should take better care of Annie and understand what Annie was trying to say instead of pushing her away and saying "nothing's wrong." Annie's mom was so worried all the time that she didn't seem to have much time for Annie anymore. Annie thought that maybe her mom didn't love her either. Often Annie thought that maybe nobody loved her at all.[9]

When Annie thought that nobody loved her at all, she felt very sad and lonely and scared. She would sit in her room and wonder why nobody loved her. She thought that maybe nobody loved her because she was such a terrible person.[10] That thought made her feel even worse. She thought that maybe it was her fault that her mom didn't take care of her and her dad drank so much. She felt terrible when she thought that, but she didn't know what to do.[11]

Often, when Annie was sitting in her room, she could hear her mother and father fighting and yelling at each other. Annie got very scared when she heard that. She was scared that they would hurt each other.[12] She was scared that maybe they'd even kill each other, and then she wouldn't have a mommy and daddy at all. She would sit there in her room getting more and more scared, and she didn't know what to do.

Sometimes Annie would look around her class at school. Everyone looked so normal. Annie was sure they all had happy normal homes with happy normal families in them; she felt certain that the other kids didn't have to be scared of their daddy's drinking, and they didn't have to keep secrets and they could bring their friends home whenever they felt like it.[13]

---

[9]Children may feel rejected by both parents in an alcoholic family. The alcoholic parent may be emotionally unavailable. The preoccupied and anxious nonalcoholic parent may also find it difficult to give children the attention they need.
[10]Children tend to believe that they are not loved because they are unlovable.
[11]Powerlessness is a common feeling among children of alcoholics.
[12]Physical violence in the family is terrifying for children.
[13]Children of alcoholics tend to idealize other families and to imagine that they are the only ones with problems.

Annie decided that the best way to stop feeling so bad was to stop feeling at all.[14] She tried not to think about her daddy's drinking. She tried not to think about not being able to talk to her mom. She did her household chores very responsibly like a big girl, and she kept out of everyone's way. Of course she couldn't keep out of everyone's way all the time, so she often got into trouble. It wasn't usually her fault, but she still got into trouble. After a while she got very good at watching people so she would know what they were going to do next.[15] That way it was easier to keep out of trouble. Sometimes Annie wished there were someone she could talk to, but she knew there was no one who would understand and no one she could trust.[16] So she just kept very quiet and watched people very carefully and tried not to feel as miserable as she was really feeling.

Thanksgiving was coming up soon. All the other kids were looking forward to it. To them it meant family dinners and fun. Annie wasn't looking forward to it at all. To her it meant family dinners and drink and fights.[17]

Maybe this time it won't be so bad, she said to herself as she went to sleep that night.

But it was bad. It was really bad. Her father got drunk and started saying stupid things. Her mom got upset. Her dad yelled at her mom. Aunt Ellen tried to pretend that it wasn't happening at all. Uncle Bob started yelling at her dad. Everyone started yelling at each other. Annie left the table as soon as she could and crawled miserably into bed. She lay awake the whole night. She wished her family were normal. She wished there were something she could do. She wished there were someone who could understand.

---

[14]Many children of alcoholics cope by putting a damper on all their feelings, both good and bad ones. This may save them from consciously experiencing intensely painful emotions, but it also prevents them from feeling the joyful ones.

[15]This is just one way of coping. If your child has adopted a different style of coping, incorporate that into the story.

[16]Because they have often been schooled in secrecy and lived with the unpredictability of the alcoholic, it is often difficult for children of alcoholics to trust people.

[17]Holiday festivities, which mean fun for most children, often spell trouble and drunken fights for the children of alcoholics.

The next morning Annie had to drag herself out of bed to go to school. She hadn't slept at all and she felt terrible.

Mrs. Rowan told them to write an essay in class; the title was "My Thanksgiving Day."

Annie sat at her desk and watched all the other kids writing. They were writing about the fun they had had at Thanksgiving dinner. They were writing about people who hugged each other and said nice things to each other. They were writing about eating turkey and cranberry sauce and just being normal.

Annie didn't have anything she wanted to write about, so she just sat there doing nothing. She noticed Mrs. Rowan looking at her now and then, but she didn't care. She sat and stared out the window while everyone wrote about their happy, normal Thanksgiving dinner and about their happy, normal families.

At the end of class, Mrs. Rowan gathered up all the essays. Everyone was just getting up to leave when Mrs. Rowan said, "Annie, would you mind staying behind, please. I'd like to have a word with you."

Now she was going to get into trouble, thought Annie. Mrs. Rowan was going to be angry because Annie hadn't written an essay. But Annie felt so miserable that she just didn't care.

"Annie," said Mrs. Rowan, and to Annie's surprise her voice sounded very kind.

Annie looked up.

"I have the feeling that something's wrong, Annie," said Mrs. Rowan. "I have the feeling that you're very unhappy."

Annie was just about to say no, because she knew she had to keep the secret, and she knew she couldn't trust anyone, and she knew no one would understand, when all of a sudden she found herself nodding yes and bursting into tears.

Mrs. Rowan patted Annie on the shoulder and said, "You're very upset, aren't you. It must be awful for you. Why don't you tell me what's wrong?"

And her voice sounded so kind and so friendly that Annie did.

She told Mrs. Rowan everything. About her father drinking and her parents fighting and her mother not having any time for Annie. It felt weird to be telling Mrs. Rowan all those things that Annie had kept secret for so long. It felt a bit scary, but it also felt good. Mrs. Rowan listened carefully to what Annie was saying. She nodded her head occasionally and looked sad, as if she really understood. And then when Annie had finished and Mrs. Rowan started speaking, Annie felt such a sense of relief. Because from what Mrs. Rowan said, Annie could tell that she really had understood.

"That must be awful for you, Annie," said Mrs. Rowan. "You must feel very alone and frightened sometimes."

Annie nodded.

"But did you know, Annie," asked Mrs. Rowan, "that lots and lots of kids have exactly the same problem with their mom or dad drinking and all of those awful things happening?"[18]

Annie's eyes opened wide. She couldn't believe this was true. She thought everyone else had normal, happy families. Not families like hers.

Mrs. Rowan nodded. "It's true," she said. "There are lots and lots of kids like you. But because they're told not to talk about it, everyone thinks they're the only one."

"Gosh," said Annie. "I'd love to meet some kids who are just like me."

"Well," said Mrs. Rowan, "there is a place where you can do just that." And she told Annie about Al Anon.[19]

"You know," said Mrs. Rowan, "maybe I could ask your mom to come to the school and have a chat. Then I can tell her all about Al Anon and you could both go."

"That would be great," said Annie. "I'd like to go somewhere like that with my mom. Then we could talk about it. She never talks about it now."[20]

"It's hard to talk about at first," said Mrs. Rowan, "but after the

---

[18] It is a great relief for children to know that there are many others like them. Often they feel as if they are the only ones with problems like this.

[19] Addresses for Al Anon and AA can probably be found in your local telephone book.

[20] Often parents don't talk about a problem in the mistaken belief that if they don't talk about it, children won't know it's there. Children invariably are aware of the problem. Talking about it helps clear up their confusion, sort out their feelings, and build bridges of support and communication.

first few times, it gets a whole lot easier, and you feel a whole lot better."

Annie nodded. "I'd like to feel a whole lot better," she said.

"Well," said Mrs. Rowan, "you've already taken the first big step by talking to me about it. That was a very hard and very important thing to do. I'm very proud of you."

Annie beamed. It felt nice to think she had done something important. "Golly," she said to Mrs. Rowan. "I didn't think there was anything I could do. I thought that nothing I could do would change things."[21]

"That's what a lot of kids feel when they have a mom or dad who drinks too much," said Mrs. Rowan. "So they don't talk to anyone or try to tell people that something's wrong. They just feel sad inside and sort of hopeless. Sometimes they even feel that maybe it's their fault that their mom or dad drinks and doesn't take care of them."

Annie nodded.

"It never is the kid's fault, though," said Mrs. Rowan. "It's not your fault that your dad drinks, and it's not your fault that your mom couldn't talk about things with you."[22]

"If Mom and I can go to Al Anon, what about my dad? Is there something my dad can do to feel better and stop drinking?" Annie asked.

"There are some things he could do." Mrs. Rowan answered. "There's a place called AA, which is for people who drink too much. There are counselors he could see to help him work things out. There are some counselors who could see your mom and dad together and some who would see the whole family. But it all depends on whether your dad is ready to do that or not. Even if he isn't ready, it doesn't mean that you can't find ways to feel happier and stronger in yourself. You can still do that anyway."[23]

"Really?" said Annie.

---

[21]Children often feel they are powerless to do anything. It's important for them to know that there are some things they can do.

[22]Children sometimes feel that it is their fault that a parent drinks.

[23]It is important for children to know that they can find ways of feeling better even though they may not be able to control their parent's drinking.

"Definitely," said Mrs. Rowan. "And like I said, you've already made the first step."

"You know," said Annie, "I used to think that I would never be happy. That things would always stay the same."

"Lots of kids think that," said Mrs. Rowan, "but it doesn't have to be true."

Mrs. Rowan looked at Annie. "I have a good idea," she said. "Let me teach you a special game I used to play when I was your age."

"What is it?" asked Annie.

"It's called the Time Leap game," said Mrs. Rowan.

"How do you play it?" asked Annie.

"You have to close your eyes and pretend you're in a time machine. See, we can both do it," and Mrs. Rowan closed her eyes.

Annie did, too. "What do we do next?" she asked.

"We have to decide how far into the future we want to go and then we dial it up on our time machine," said Mrs. Rowan.

"Okay," said Annie. She thought for a minute. "I'm going to dial up fifteen years."

"Hold onto your seat," said Mrs. Rowan, "we're zooming forward fifteen years in time."

"Wow," said Annie.

"I think we're here," said Mrs. Rowan. "Do you want to see what fifteen years into the future looks like? Hey! I can see you. You look terrific. You're all grown up. You have a really big smile on your face."

"I can see me, too," said Annie. "I'm in my apartment. I have a really neat apartment all of my own," she said proudly.[24]

"There are a lot of books around your apartment," said Mrs. Rowan.

"That's because I'm a writer," said Annie. "A writer has to read a lot of books."

---

[24]For children who feel powerless and stuck in an untenable family situation, this "Time-Leap" enables them to see that there is a future in which they can extricate themselves and make positive choices. It gives them goals to plan for and, most importantly, a sense of hope.

"What sort of writing do you do?" asked Mrs. Rowan.

Annie thought for a moment. Then she had a great idea. "I wrote a big best selling book last year," she said.

"Wow," said Mrs. Rowan. "What was it about?"

"It was all about how to help kids whose mom or dad drank too much. It helped lots of kids."

"That sounds terrific," said Mrs. Rowan.

"It sure was," said Annie. "It was great."

"I bet," said Mrs. Rowan. And then she looked at her watch. "But I have the feeling that it's almost time to get back to the present, so we'd better dial the time machine back to where we started."

Annie opened her eyes. "Here we are back in the present," she said. She was smiling.

"That's right," said Mrs. Rowan. "Now, before you head off to wherever you're going, do you want to set up a time to see me in a few days so we can talk some more?"

"That would be great," said Annie. She felt better than she had felt in a long time. For the first time, she felt that something good might happen.

A week later Annie's mom said to her, "Would you like to go for a walk to the park with me, Annie?"

Annie was surprised. "Sure," she said.

They walked along in the sunshine. Annie's mom took her hand and they swung their hands up and down as they walked.

"I went to have a talk with Mrs. Rowan yesterday," said her mom.

"Oh," said Annie. She felt suddenly frightened, worried about what her mom was going to say next.

Annie's mom put her arm around her and gave her a great big hug.

"Mrs. Rowan told me how unhappy you'd been. She told me how miserable you felt about Dad's drinking and the way our family's been lately."

Annie looked up at her mom.

"I'm really very sorry, honey," said her mom. "I guess I thought that if I didn't talk about it, maybe you wouldn't know it was happening."

Annie looked sad. "No, Mom," she said, "I knew what was happening."

"Poor Annie," said her mom. "It must have been hard for you."

Annie nodded.

"I wish there had been something I could do to make it better for you," said her mom.

"There was," said Annie.

Her mom looked at her.

"If you could have hugged me and talked to me like you're doing now, that would have made it better," said Annie.

"You know Annie, you're right," said her mom and gave her another hug. "I guess I got so worried about it all that I wasn't thinking straight." She looked at Annie. "But now that I know, maybe we can start from now on and do it better."

Annie smiled. "That would be great," she said.

# 14

# Relaxation

We all need to relax. Some of us are good at it, while others find it hard to do. Children are the same. Relaxation makes almost everything feel better and run more smoothly. We feel less pain when we are relaxed, we work better, play more happily, feel healthier, sleep more easily, and in general function at a significantly more enjoyable level.

Children can benefit from relaxation when they're stressed, overtired, frustrated, worried, overexcited, or when they simply feel like it. Just as with adults, many children have to be taught how to relax or reminded when to do it.

Teaching relaxation through the medium of storytelling is a particularly pleasant method, both for the child and the storyteller. Some children like an active fantasy in which a lot happens. Others like a more passive one in which they may just sit quietly in a peaceful scene with nothing much going on. Children's wants and needs differ from time to time as well as from child to child.

It can be helpful to teach children muscle relaxation. One way of doing this, for instance, is to get your child to imagine that she is turning, bit by bit, into a rag doll. Start with, say, the left hand and see how floppy it can get. Then move on to the left arm and so on until you've been all around the body. Do this alongside your child so that you are modeling the technique for her. You might even have a little "competition" to see who can get floppiest. An example of this is given in Chapter 11, Impulsive Children.

You can also help children relax by engaging their imagination. Getting them to imagine themselves doing something pleasant can ease them into a relaxed state. You might want to try a fantasy similar to the one I've used in the Annie Story dealing with pain in

the first book. In that story Annie takes an imaginary trip to
Playland. In Playland, it's always your birthday and you're always
special and everyone plays the games that you want to play. There
are magic carousel horses and picture shows where you can get
inside the screen and be part of the adventure. There are spaghetti
trees that also grow their own sauce. There are chocolate trees and
lollipop flowers. And there's the Anything Bush which grows anything you want it to. There's a games section of Playland where
you can join in any game you could possibly think of. There are
Birthday Cake shops and Present Machines. And after all the
partying, there are special Dream Beds to lie down and rest on.

Suit the fantasy to your child. If your child wants to be a cham-
pionship horseback rider, for instance, you might get her to imagine riding in a very fast and exciting horse race. Afterwards, still
in her imagination, she can settle her horse down and have a well-
deserved rest herself.

When you're describing these scenes, make them as rich in detail
as possible so that the imagery is vivid and alive. Whenever possible, describe the feel, sound, smell, and taste of the scene as well
as the way it looks. These extra descriptive dimensions add to the
vitality and intensity of the experience.

As you tell the following story, your child may spontaneously
start to comment on her own fantasy scenes with the carpet. It's
helpful to listen encouragingly to these and perhaps weave them
into the story or into future stories. Don't be dismayed by her
talking—she can still be relaxed as she speaks, and it shows that
she is entering wholeheartedly into the story. The more involved
your child is, the more she will gain from it. It may be helpful to
suggest to your child that she can enjoy listening to the story even
more with her eyes closed.

In this story, Annie's mother tells her a story about a little girl
called Andrea. The technique of telling a story within a story and
confusing the boundaries between the two can serve to increase
the child's involvement and help with the relaxation process.

# annie story

Annie was a little girl who lived in a brown brick house with her mommy and daddy and a big black dog.[1]

Usually she woke up each morning feeling happy and sunny, but one day when she woke up, it was with a cross, grumpy feeling. It was a feeling she didn't like.[2]

She stomped into the kitchen. "Where's my breakfast," she demanded of her mother.

"My goodness," said her mother, "you look as if you got up on the wrong side of bed this morning."

"A big nasty motorcycle roared by in the street before I was ready to wake up. I didn't want to wake up, but it made me wake up,"said Annie. She was very cross about it. She thought all motorcycles ought to be scrunched up and fed to a big motorcycle-eating monster.

"Well, here are your cornflakes, darling," said her mom. "I've got them all ready for you."

"I don't want cornflakes, I want crispies," snapped Annie.

"Well, darling, I'm sorry about that, but I've already poured the milk. You can have crispies tomorrow."

"I don't want crispies tomorrow, I want them today. It's not fair!" said Annie, and she marched into the TV room. "You should have asked me before you poured them."

In the TV room she looked at the TV guide and then she looked at the clock. Darn it! She had missed her favorite TV show. It was just not fair.[3]

"I've missed my TV show," she wailed to her mother. "You should have woken me up. It's not fair!"

"I'm sorry, darling," said her mom, giving her shoulder a pat, "but I didn't know you wanted to watch it. Why don't you play with your new jigsaw puzzle instead."

---

[1] Tailor these details to fit in with your child's environment.

[2] This provides the motivation for Annie's wish to learn relaxation—it will help her feel better and enjoy the day more.

[3] Tailor these upsetting events to fit your child's situation so that she can identify with them.

Annie looked around. Her new puzzle was lying on the coffee table. It was a big, shiny puzzle with pictures of hamsters on it. Annie loved hamsters.[4] She had never actually met a hamster, but she had watched "The Adventures of Hammy Hamster and His Friends on the Riverbank" on TV and she knew she would just love a hamster if she found one. Last night she had asked her mom and dad to buy her a hamster, but her dad had said, "No. One dog in this house is quite enough. And besides, who'd look after it? Definitely no hamsters until you're old enough to look after them yourself." It wasn't fair, thought Annie. All she wanted was one little hamster.

"Why don't you get dressed first?" asked her mom. "It's a bit cold in here with just your nightie on."

Annie went to her room. She knew just what she wanted to wear today—her favorite red sweat-suit. She looked in her cupboard.

"My sweat-suit's not here!" she said to her mother.

"It's in the wash," said her mom. "Why don't you pick out something else?"

"I don't want to wear something else. I want to wear my sweat-suit," said Annie. "It's not fair." And she stomped back into the TV room.

She had just organized the jigsaw puzzle into a pile of the straight-edged pieces that went on the sides, and a pile of all the others, when Blackie, the dog, walked in. Now, Blackie loved three things in life—she loved playing fetch, going for walks, and eating tissues and jigsaw puzzle pieces.

She came in very quietly so that Annie didn't hear her. Slowly her wet nose began to sniff, sniff, sniff at the table where the jigsaw pieces were. She really loved tissues best, but jigsaw pieces would do, so suddenly, with a quick snatch, she grabbed three pieces and ran off down the hall.

Annie ran after her, yelling, "Bad dog! Bad dog! Give me back my jigsaw pieces!"

Annie's mom came around the corner, grabbed Blackie, and took

---

[4]My daughter currently has a hankering for hamsters, so I've made use of this in the story. You can make similar use of your own child's fads and fancies.

the pieces from her mouth. "Here you are," she said to Annie. "Here are your jigsaw pieces."

"They're all wet!" said Annie. "Yuk! It's not fair!" She felt like crying.

"You're really having a rotten morning, aren't you," said her mom. Annie nodded.

"And you feel just terrible," her mom went on.[5]

"Yes," said Annie. "I feel rotten. It's a rotten day."

"Would you like me to show you a way of feeling better?" asked her mom. "That way you might at least be able to enjoy the rest of the day and it wouldn't be such a waste for you."[6]

"Okay," said Annie, "I'd like that. How would I do it?"

"Well, sit down and let me tell you a special story," said her mom, "and as you listen to the story, you might begin to feel better and better."

"Okay," said Annie. This sounded good.

Annie got settled comfortably and her mom began.

"Once upon a time, there was a little girl called Andrea. Normally she was a happy little girl, but today she had been having a horrible, horrible day. Everything she did went wrong. Her lunch was a yucky lunch, her drawings didn't work out right, and her favorite storybook was missing.[7]

"'I feel yucky,' she said to her mom. 'I'm having a horrible day.'

"'Would you like to know how to feel better?' asked her mom.

"'I certainly would,' said Andrea, because she didn't like feeling yucky like this. 'How do I do it?'

"'Well,' said Andrea's mom, 'why don't you sit down comfortably, and I'll show you how to do some very special breathing that will help you feel better. We can just sit here and take some very quiet, deep breaths. They're very special breaths because it's a very

---

[5]This sort of response enables your child to feel listened to and understood. She is then likely to feel more ready to listen to your suggestions.

[6]This provides some motivation for your child—at least the rest of the day won't be such a waste.

[7]Andrea's upsetting situations are similar to Annie's. This enables the child to identify easily with Andrea as well as with Annie. Again, suit these situations to your own child's experience.

special, magical way of breathing. I'll explain to you why that is in a minute.'"[8]

And then Annie's mom said to Annie.[9] "You can breath along with me and Andrea and her mom, too, if you like, and then you can be part of the special, magical breathing."

"Oh, great," said Annie. She had been going to do that anyway, even if her mom hadn't said it.

"Then," Annie's mom went on, "Andrea's mom said, 'Now we can just sit here and breathe quietly for a few minutes, and feel the breath coming in and going all through our bodies, filling us up with air and then coming out again.'

"'Yes, I can feel that,' said Andrea."

"I can feel that too," said Annie. She was enjoying breathing and listening to the story. She was waiting to hear what the special, magical part of this breathing was. She liked things that were special and magical.

"'Now, the special, magical part of this breathing,' went on Andrea's mom, 'is that if you close your eyes and imagine looking very closely, you can see the special breaths as they go through your body. When the breath comes in, it's clear and sparkling, like light or glass. As it goes through your body, it changes color. By the time it goes out of your body, it's very gray or muddy.'[10]

"'Ooh, I can see it now,' said Andrea. She had her eyes closed and she could imagine seeing the breath coming in and going out of her body, very slowly, because she was breathing very slowly and quietly.

"'What color is it?' asked her mom.

"'When it comes in, it's a lovely sparkling white, like a diamond. When it goes out, it's yucky brown.'"

"I can see mine too," said Annie. She also had her eyes closed

---

[8]Children love things that are special or magical—their interest is immediately captured.

[9]The Annie and Andrea stories are becoming interwoven here as they will continue to be for the rest of the story. This double interweaving can allow your child to become more fully absorbed by the story.

[10]Your child might volunteer what the color of her breath is here, or you might like to ask her what she imagines it would be like.

and was breathing quietly. "It's white when it comes in and it's a muddy color when it goes out."

"'Why does it change color?' asked Andrea.

"'It changes color,' said her mom, 'because as it travels through your body, it's picking up all the bad feelings and all the rotten things that have happened to you during the day, and it's taking them away with it, outside your body.'

"'You mean like a sponge does when you wipe up messes on the table?' asked Andrea.

"'That's right,' said her mom. 'And just like a sponge, the more we wipe up, the less yucky stuff is left. If you look at your breath coming out now, for instance, you would probably see that it's not quite as brown as it was before.'

"'That's right," said Andrea."

"It's happening to me too," said Annie. "This is great."

"'And as you keep watching your breath," Andrea's mom said, 'you can see that it keeps on getting lighter and clearer as it goes out. That's because there's less and less yucky stuff left in you. All the bad feelings and rotten things that happened to you today are being cleared away by the magic breaths.'

"'This is great,' said Andrea. 'My breath's nearly completely clear now.'"

"Mine's clear already," said Annie. "It cleared up even faster than Andrea's. It's white all the way through. This is terrific. It feels really good. I like this."

"That's great," said Annie's mom. She went on, "And Andrea's mom said, 'Tell me when your breath is completely clear, then we can do something more that you'll really enjoy.'

"'It's clear now,' said Andrea.

"Andrea's mother continued, 'That's great. Now we can go on a very special magic trip in our imagination. And it's something that you can really enjoy.'

"'What is it?' asked Andrea. She was really looking forward to this. She loved magic trips.

"'It's a trip on your very own magic carpet,' said her mom.

"'Oh, wow!' said Andrea."

"'Oh, goodie," said Annie. She had always wanted to take a trip on a magic carpet, but she hadn't known that you could do that in your mind.

"'You can do anything in your mind,' said Andrea's mom. 'Because it's your mind and your imagination, you can control it. You can make anything happen that you like. You can change anything that you like. And everything that happens can feel just right, just comfortable for you.'

"'Oh, wow,' said Andrea."

"This is going to be great," said Annie. She was really looking forward to this.

"'First of all," said Andrea's mom, 'you have to choose what color your magic carpet will be. Will it be pink or red or yellow or blue? Will it be green or purple or black or white? Will it be just one color or different colors?'[11]

"Andrea thought for a few moments."

Annie thought, too. It was funny how it was easier to think of these things when you had your eyes closed. She began to see lovely colors floating across her mind. Which of them would she choose? . . . [12]

"'I'll have purple and white,' announced Andrea, and she imagined a beautiful purple and white carpet. 'Purple is for princes and princesses, and I like that.'"

"My carpet will be white and purple," said Annie, and she imagined a wonderful white and purple carpet for herself. "White is for unicorns, and I like that."

"'What sort of pattern does your carpet have?' asked Andrea's mom. 'Are they swirly, circle patterns or are they straight, square patterns? Are they simple, separate patterns or are they all tangled up patterns? Or are they no patterns at all? . . .'

"Andrea looked closely at her carpet. It had a lovely pattern of white moons on a purple background.

---

[11]This imaginative exercise involves the visual sense—what do you see, what does it look like, etc. The more senses you can bring into play, the more vivid the imagery becomes. Other senses are called up as the story continues.

[12]A pause here allows your child time to meditate on what color her carpet will be. Whenever you see a series of dots ( . . . ) in this story, pause for a moment or two before going on.

"'I've got moons on my carpet,' she said. 'They're beautiful.'"

Annie looked closely at her carpet, too. It was lovely. It had a beautiful pattern of purple stars on a white background.

"I love my carpet," she said. "It has purple stars on it."

"'That sounds beautiful,' said Andrea's mom.

"'That sounds beautiful," said Annie's mom, and she continued. "Andrea's mom said, 'What does your carpet feel like, I wonder? Is it smooth and silky, or is it soft and furry? Is it cool like sheets, or warm like blankets?[13] I wonder what nice feeling your carpet has for you? . . ."

"'Mine's warm and woolly,' said Andrea. "I can snuggle up in it.'"

"Mine's comfortable and cozy," said Annie. "I can cuddle up in it."

"'That sounds nice,' said Andrea's mom. 'Now, where do you think you'd like to fly in it? Would you like to fly somewhere special, or would you like to just fly around in the sky over the rooftops for a while? . . ."

"Andrea thought for a moment. 'I think I just feel like floating around in the sky for a while,' she said.

"'That sounds nice,' said her mom."

"I might just want to fly around and see what I can see," said Annie.

"I think you'll enjoy that," said her mom.

"'I wonder how fast your magic carpet will fly?' asked Andrea's mom. 'Will it whoosh along like a jet plane, or will it just ease along gently, drifting here and there? Will it fly in a straight line or will it curve around in circles? . . .'

"'I'm not sure,' said Andrea. 'I might just fly around wherever I feel like.'"

"Me, too," said Annie. She was enjoying this. It was nice flying around on a magic carpet.

"'What might you hear, I wonder, on your magic carpet?' asked Andrea's mom.[14] 'Some magic carpets sing songs, you know. Some sing music without words and some sing words without music.

---

[13]This involves the tactile sense—how does it feel, how do you feel, etc.

[14]This involves the auditory sense—what do you hear, what does it sound like, etc.

Some talk to you when you want them to, as you whoosh through the sky, and some are peacefully quiet . . .'

"'Mine's singing nursery rhymes,' said Andrea. She was surprised."

"Mine's singing my favorite music," said Annie. "I don't know what it's called, but I like it."

"'It's nice to fly on a magic carpet,' said Andrea's mom. 'You can fly over beaches and cities and fields. You can fly over mountains and meadows and trees. You can fly over deserts and lakes and snowfields. Where will you fly, I wonder . . .'"

"Andrea didn't answer for a few minutes. She was too busy seeing all there was to see. Then she said, 'I'm flying over meadows and grass and trees. There are rabbits and squirrels. I can see them frolicking in the leaves.'"

"I'm flying over everything," said Annie. She wanted to see it all.

"'It feels nice, doesn't it, on your magic carpet,' said Andrea's mom. 'Magic carpets are happy carpets and anyone who sits on them feels happy. It's part of their magic.'"

"'I feel happy,' said Andrea."

"I feel very happy," said Annie. She was enjoying this. It was a bit like being on a ship at sea. The wind was like the waves and there was a gentle breeze . . .

"After a while, Andrea's mom said, 'Now you might like to look around and find a lovely place to land and rest for a while. You can find a place that looks just right for you. A place that's smiling and peaceful and just what you like . . .'"

"Andrea looked around and then she found just the right spot. 'I've found it,' she said. 'It's wonderful.'"

"I've found my place, too," said Annie. "It's pretty. It's green and peaceful, and there are flowers in the meadow. And," she gave a gasp of surprise, "there are hamsters in the meadow, too. They're running up to me now. They want to play at my feet, and then they want to sleep in my lap. Oh, wow, this is great!'[15]

---

[15]The hamsters, or something else your child loves, are a special little treat here to make the experience even more enjoyable.

"That's terrific," said her mom. "You can play with them as much as you like, and then you can all rest. You and the hamsters."

"It's beautiful," said Annie, after a while. "I'm resting now."

"You can have a long rest," said her mom. "You don't have to sleep, but you can sit there and look around. There are such lovely things to see, and you can feel that everything's just right. It's such a comfortable feeling, to know that everything's just right. It's just the way you'd like it to be . . . [16]

"'Now,' said Andrea's mom, 'soon you can get ready to say goodbye-for-now to your carpet.[17] You're not saying goodbye forever because you can come back for another trip whenever you like. Now, though, you are getting ready to be back here with me. And you can take with you that happy, peaceful feeling the carpet gave you. It can stay with you, and whatever you're doing can feel especially wonderful.[18] You might imagine yourself now, getting up and doing whatever it is you're going to be doing after this.[19] And whatever it is that you're going to be doing, you can imagine yourself feeling really good doing it. It feels really lovely. And it feels nice to know that it will feel so good . . ."

"'I'm going to be doing some drawing after this,' said Andrea dreamily. 'I'll really enjoy it.'"

"I'm going to be doing my jigsaw puzzle," said Annie. "I can see myself doing it now. I feel really good."

"'Good,' said Andrea's mom. 'Now you can see yourself opening your eyes with a happy smile and feeling just so nice . . .'

"Andrea opened her eyes. 'Gee, that was fun," she said."

Annie opened her eyes. "It's great flying on a magic carpet," she said, and she gave her mom a hug. "I feel really good. I think I'm going to have a great, great day."[20]

---

[16] You can extend this resting time for as long as you like.

[17] Let your child know that she is able to recapture this experience at another time when it might be helpful for her to relax.

[18] Emphasize that this relaxed feeling can stay with her even after she is no longer in the daydream.

[19] This is particularly useful when your child's next activity is likely to be something stressful, difficult, or frustrating. The positive visualization of herself completing this task with equanimity helps promote this attitude in real life.

[20] This is the positive ending.

# Resources

**Family Information Services,** 12565 Jefferson Street NE, Suite 102, Minneapolis, MN 55434. Phone: 612-755-6233

**Alcoholics Anonymous,** P.O. Box 459, Grand Central Station, New York, NY 10163-1100. Phone: 216-686-1100

**Al-Anon/Alateen Family Group Headquarters,** P.O. Box 862, Midtown Station, New York, NY 10018-0862. Phone: 212-302-7240

**Obsessive-Compulsive Disorders Foundation,** P.O. Box 9573, New Haven, CT 06535. Phone: 203-772-0565

**Simon Foundation for Continence,** P.O. Box 835, Wilmette, IL 60091. Phone: 800-23-SIMON patient information, 708-864-3913 foundation headquarters

**Stepfamily Foundation,** 333 West End Avenue, New York, NY 10023. Phone: 212-877-3244

# Further Reading

**Chapters 1, 2, and 3**
Doris Brett, *Annie Stories*, Workman, New York, 1988.
Stella Chess and Alexander Thomas, *Know Your Child: An Authoritative Guide for Today's Parents*, Basic Books, New York, 1989.
Selma H. Fraiberg, *The Magic Years: Understanding and Handling the Problems of Early Childhood*, Macmillan, New York, 1966.
Julius Segan and Herbert Yahraes, *A Child's Journey: Forces that Shape the Lives of Our Young*, McGraw-Hill, New York, 1979.

**4 Fear of the Dark**
Richard Ferber, *Solve Your Child's Sleep Problems*, Simon & Schuster, New York, 1986.
Montague Ullman and Nan Zimmerman, *Working with Dreams: Self-Understanding, Problem-Solving, and Enriched Creativity Through Dream Appreciation*, J. P. Tarcher, Los Angeles, 1985.

**5 Bedwetting**
Martin B. Scharf, *Waking Up Dry: How to End Bedwetting Forever*, Writer's Digest Books, Cincinnati, 1986.

**6 Compulsive and Perfectionistic Children**
Judith Rapoport, *The Boy Who Couldn't Stop Washing: The Experience and Treatment of Obsessive-Compulsive Disorder.* New American Library-Dutton, New York, 1991.

**7 Shyness**
Gwendolyn Cartledge and JoAnne Milburn (Editors), *Teaching Social Skills to Children: Innovative Approaches*, Pergamon, Elmsford, NY, 1986.
Philip Zimbardo, *Shyness*, Addison-Wesley, Redding, MA, 1990.

**8 Teasing**
Stephen W. Garber, Marianne Daniels Garber and Robyn Freedman Spizman, *Good Behavior: Over 1200 Sensible Solutions to Your Child's Problems.* Random House, New York, 1987.

**9 Divorce**
Eda Le Shan, *What's Going to Happen to Me? When Parents Separate or Divorce*, Macmillan, New York, 1986.
Judith S. Wallerstein and Sandra Blakeslee, *Second Chances: Men, Women and Children a Decade After Divorce*, Tichnor & Fields, New York, 1990.
Judith S. Wallerstein and Joan B. Kelly, *Surviving the Breakup: How Children and Parents Cope with Divorce*, Basic Books, New York, 1990.

**10 Stepfamilies**
Emily B. Visher and John S. Visher, *Stepfamilies: A Guide to Working with Stepparents and Stepchildren*, Brunner/Mazel, New York, 1979.

**11 Impulsive Children**
Philip C. Kendall and Lauren Braswell, *Cognitive-Behavioral Therapy for Impulsive Children*, Guilford Press, New York, 1984.
D. Meichenbaum and J. Goodman, "Training Impulsive Children to Talk to Themselves: A Means of Developing Self-Control, *Journal of Abnormal Psychology*, Vol. 77, pp. 115–126, 1971.
Myrna B. Shure and George Spivack, *Problem-Solving Techniques in Childrearing*, Books on Demand UMI, Ann Arbor, MI, 1978.

**12 Siblings**
Adele Faber and Elaine Mazlish, *Siblings Without Rivalry: How to Help Your Children Live Together So You Can Live Too*, W. W. Norton, New York, 1987.

**13 Children of Alcoholics**
Robert J. Ackerman, *Children of Alcoholics: A Guide for Parents, Educators and Therapists*, 3rd edition, Simon & Schuster, New York, 1987.
Robert J. Ackerman, *Same House, Different Homes: Why Adult Children of Alcoholics Are Not All the Same*, Health Communications, Deerfield, FL, 1987.
Claudia Black, *My Dad Loves Me, My Dad Has a Disease*, Medical Administration Company, Denver, 1982.
Sharon Wegscheider and R. W. Esterly, *Alcoholism and the Family: A Book of Readings*, Caron Institute, Wernersville, PA 1985.

**14 Relaxation**
Stephen W. Garber, Marianne Daniels Garber, and Robyn Freedman Spizman, *Good Behavior: Over 1200 Sensible Solutions to Your Child's Problems*, Random House, 1987.